SUCCESSFUL FAILURE

SUCCESSFUL
FAILURE

LESSONS LEARNED
FLAT ON MY FACE

KEVIN
FREDERICKS

CONVERGENT
NEW YORK

Convergent
An imprint of Random House
A division of Penguin Random House LLC
1745 Broadway, New York, NY 10019
convergentbooks.com
penguinrandomhouse.com

Hardback ISBN 9780593735671
Ebook ISBN 9780593735688

Printed in the United States of America on acid-free paper

2 4 6 8 9 7 5 3 1

First Edition

Editor: Derek Reed • Editorial assistant: Ashley Shoemaker •
Production editor: Loren Noveck • Managing editor: Allie Fox •
Production manager: Chanler Harris • Copy editor: David Goehring •
Proofreaders: Erika Bruner, Anya Getschel, and Rachel Twersky

Book design by Diane Hobbing

The authorized representative in the EU for product safety and compliance
is Penguin Random House Ireland, Morrison Chambers, 32 Nassau Street,
Dublin D02 YH68, Ireland. https://eu-contact.penguin.ie.

I dedicate this to my brother, Jason. I love and miss you every day. Brothers in arms.

CONTENTS

INTRODUCTION

I first saw the signs as a child.

I can't remember when I happened upon the first one, but even then, as a kid barely older than ten, I knew precisely what those signs meant for me. They signaled that I was preordained to be so much more than what the world expected of a little Black boy from working-class West Texas. I was meant to be big! And each time I saw the signs—on TV or on family trips or in print—I grew ever more convinced. The signs called to me constantly, blaring my destiny with loud, brazen, neon assuredness:

Frederick's of Hollywood!

I mean, what else could that stand for, right?

Okay, so yeah, I found out later that it stood for silky lingerie and skimpy drawers—but back then, I ain't know that! As a kid growing up with vague hopes of being some sort of entertainer one day, those Frederick's of Hollywood signs were my North Star, a sure indicator that my dreams would eventually be realized and my life would be defined by legitimate success.

The "dreams come true" part was accurate. As of this writing, I've done multiple comedy tours that have been sold out in churches and other venues across the United States and the world. I've got enough followers on X, YouTube, and Instagram combined to populate a major city. I've got a TV show that airs on a major streaming service. I'm in a loving marriage that has produced two wonderful sons and a bestselling book. I've done promotional work for OnStar, Bevel, McDonald's, Walgreens, and a bunch of other big-name companies. I'm earning more money than ever before.

But what the signs didn't predict was that on the way to that success, I would walk a long, hard path littered with flops, fools errands, fizzles, and straight-up failures.

As much as anything else, my victories in life accrue from all the many times that I've fallen down, screwed up, acted too hastily, and rejected sage advice. Oh, I've learned some lessons all right, painful lessons that were wholly avoidable in some cases. But if there's any single reason (outside of faith and family) why I've won, it's because of, not in spite of, the fact that I've so often lost.

Failure has humbled me. Failure has inspired as well as frustrated me. Failure has made me laugh and cry, rage and sigh. But most of all, failure has been my constant teacher, an abundant source for any number of life lessons (and laughs) that continue to direct my journey and shape my perspective.

To be clear, I have failed—but I am not a failure. First, I'm doing what I love. Whether it's creating and producing my TV series or shooting a video with my friends or barnstorming through the stand-up circuit, I am fulfilling my deepest passions. Second, I'm getting better because of failure. Like Thomas Edison trying repeatedly to make his first light bulb work, I continue to toil at my craft, touring constantly, editing videos late into the night, tinkering with jokes here, overhauling punchlines there. Not only do I not quit, but I make a point of adapting to adversity as I move forward.

I'm not being defined by failure. I'm being developed by it.

And despite any success I now enjoy, I have no doubt that I will be failing again in the not too distant future. Matter of fact, now that I think of it, I'm failing right now, as I write this! True story: My team on my TV series, *Churchy,* is mad at me right this very moment because I just cost us a ton of money trying to book a location for a shoot. The location fee that was supposed to be somewhere around $2,000 or $3,000 a day went up to $15,000 because I forgot to get a firm quote. I misunderstood what the site rep was saying, so a shoot that was supposed to cost $12,000 for a few days came in at $60,000. And it's 100 percent my fault. I should've hired a location manager, but I made the mistake of thinking I could handle more of the show than I can. If I had a location manager, he or she would've had the time to follow up and get a quote and would've known what the site was going to cost. We could have found another place. I didn't budget for that and thought I could do it myself. I messed up.

But messing up is also how we get things done. One of the directors of photography I work with starts off every shoot by saying, "Okay, y'all, let's go make some mistakes." Not "Let's go shoot" or "Let's go have fun." *Let's go make some mistakes.* Him saying that sets a great tone. That kind of thinking allows you to prepare yourself to fail, because you don't even know what mistakes you are going to make until you make them. All you can really hope for is that you don't make the same mistakes over and over (which I do as well).

When my show comes out, all people are going to see is how funny it is and how great it is. They're not going to see the myriad mistakes that I've gone through. You don't learn anything, really, from doing things right. You learn how to be good by doing things wrong. You learn how to throw touchdowns because you first threw interceptions and incompletions.

I can't speak to anyone else's life, but for me, there simply is no success without failure.

Nah, hold up. Actually, I *will* speak to others' lives, at least to a degree: *You're going to fail, too.* Chances are, you probably have failed at something already. Matter of fact, you might be failing at that thing right now while you're reading this. Maybe you're struggling to lose weight or taking too long to pick up a new skill. Maybe you're not finding your ideal job, or maybe you've sucked thus far at that small business you've always dreamed of running. Failure is universal. Failure in this life is like Thanos before the Snap: It is inevitable. But what distinguishes those who stay mired in disappointment from those of us who wade through and find success is the willingness to embrace failure, accept its certainty, adapt to its lessons—and understand that failure doesn't mark the finish line.

Look, the biggest reason I wanted to write this book is to make you laugh. A lifetime of strange encounters, weird mishaps, and personal flubs is recounted in these pages, and I'd like to think you'll get a kick out of at least some of them. So laugh with me. Laugh *at* me.

But beyond that, I'm also sharing my story to dispel some misguided ideas I've seen take hold as my generation makes its mad dash to secure the bag. Podcasts, books, YouTube vlogs, and any number of other media are brimming with false ideas about success, creating illusory impressions that it can be achieved overnight or that it can be measured by the commas and zeroes on a paycheck. We talk about hustling and grinding as though simply *doing* will automatically translate into accomplishment.

I'm here to remind you that, no matter how talented or lucky or connected you are, you will absolutely fall flat on your face at some point. And yes, you should get back up, but on your way back up, you'd better take the time to appreciate why you fell in the first place. No, failure doesn't have to mark the finish, but every bump in the road should bring deeper respect for the journey and thoughtful consideration about the direction you're headed—and maybe a little self-awareness, too. Failure isn't the end, but neither is success. Each of our journeys is a unique and continuous movement through this life, bringing new stages, fresh challenges, and plenty of setbacks. None of it is easy to navigate.

Which is why you really need to pay attention to the signs.

PART ONE

Aimless Ambition

THE SHOW MUST GO ON

I never saw the rock coming—which makes sense since it was make-believe—but I was ready for it all the same.

I was about seven years old and standing onstage with my older brother, Jason, at our family's church in El Paso, Texas. Together, in front of our entire congregation, Jay and I were acting out our own updated comedic version of the David and Goliath story. We'd spent weeks writing and revising our little script, loading it up with as much cool hip hop lingo as two Pentecostal boys could get away with in a West Texas house of worship. Jay was playing David. I was giving my best urban Goliath. Both of us were determined to wow the audience.

"Can't touch this!" I shouted at my brother as we prepared to square off. (Look, MC Hammer was a big deal back then, okay? And that line got a LAUGH.) We bantered a little bit more, then Jay drew back his arm and fired a pretend stone right at my head. I prepared for impact.

When Jason and I first imagined our skit, I'd thought briefly about doing a fake pratfall, just teetering over slowly and then catching myself and easing my way to the floor. But nope. Even before my brother fired that invisible rock, I had decided that my fall had to be 100 percent convincing and, above all, entertaining. You think I cared that this was just some little skit my brother and I had put together for our church family? Oh no. It was my time to shine. I wanted—needed—to get that real audience reaction. So a half second after Jay fired his slingshot, I collapsed with as much drama as I could muster. This wasn't some lightweight tumble. I dropped fast, crumpling to my knees first before keeling over and outright face-planting, my head slamming hard onto the thin carpet that covered our church's concrete floor.

My bottom lip split wide open. Blood gushed from my mouth like an oil geyser. Goliath was down! And if the blood squirting from my mouth was any indication, he might not be getting up. Good thing my eyes were already closed, because I was hurt for real.

Then I heard it. The crowd began to clap. Cheers and peals of laughter floated from the pews. Suddenly, as I lay there, head pounding, eyes closed, lip bloodied, the pain of my awkward fall began to give way to a deep sense of satisfaction. Even at seven, I was willing to commit as fully and go as hard as I could if it meant winning over an audience. Then as now, the applause and the shouts of approval were equal parts salve, motivation, and validation.

In my own way, I knew even then that I was meant to entertain. And I would happily give everything I had to be good at it—no matter how much I'd have to bleed, no matter how many times or how hard I'd have to fall.

To some, my spill may have looked like a blooper, a flop in every sense of the word. For me, it was confirmation that I'd found my passion. I didn't care who laughed at me. Honestly, I get a kick out of that recollection myself, recalling how crazy I looked with my goofy little smile beaming proudly through blood-smeared teeth as we took our closing bows. So laugh as much as you want. It's okay. But I can only pray that you find that thing in your life that you love so much—that you desire so deeply to excel at—that you're willing to bust your face wide open . . . then get up and do it again.

ALL IN THE FAMILY

I came by all of it naturally, of course: the desire to perform, the fearlessness about falling, the determination to keep rising.

I'd entered the world as part of a devoutly Christian family that viewed entertaining church audiences as a calling, a chance to play a small part in the larger worship service. Everybody had their thing. My brother played the drums. My grandma sang in the choir. My mom was a great writer. My granddad—who ended up having another family after he and my grandma divorced—he and everyone on his side of the family were gospel artists who put out their own music. Sure, we were amateurs who never took our performances any further than church sanctuaries—nobody was going to confuse the Fredericks family for the Winanses—but each of us savored our chance to praise God with as much passion, creativity, and flair as possible. Then there was the social cachet that came with getting onstage. In our church, you were cool if you got to be a part of the service, as opposed to just being there.

Before I realized I could stand onstage and make people laugh, my first real aspiration had been to be a drummer like Jay. I loved playing drums in the church services. But Jason was so much better. Later, I discovered that I was more talented at the guitar, so I switched my interest and threw myself wholly into becoming a great bass player. I went so far as to find a mentor to teach me. He was an incredible bass player, one of the best in our community. But whenever I'd ask him to show me how he did certain things, he would just shrug, look at me, and go, "Brother, I don't know what I be doing. I just be playing. It just comes to me."

Whatever "it" was, it had clearly decided to skip over me entirely. I was never going to be a great musician. As a drummer, I washed out early. As a guitarist, I was . . . serviceable, at best. Maybe I might've gotten to "good" if I'd kept at it—but when real bass players would show up at church? It was like that old Katt Williams joke where he talks about Chrysler 300 drivers who compare their ride to a Rolls-Royce Phantom. *"Yeah, it looks like a Phantom . . . until a Phantom pulls up!"* That's how I was as a guitarist. I was cool for my church, but anytime we went to another church for the 3:30 service, you could automatically tell who the real bass player was. And it was not me.

I kept at it for a while, even into adulthood. But after Melissa and I married and had our first son, Isaiah, I gave up. I'd be trying to practice, but Zay Zay'd make it nearly impossible. He would unplug my bass from the amplifier. He'd pull at the bass strings. I was like, *I'm not going to be the world's greatest bass player, and he's not going to let me be even just an okay bass player. Maybe I'm going to be done with this.* Eventually, I just stopped.

Honestly, that's a problem of mine: If I'm not going to be the greatest at something, I lose interest. I don't just quit at something that I want, but I also don't want to squander time and energy working to be only mediocre at something. You don't have to be a huge success at something to appreciate or enjoy it, just like you don't have to be a miserable failure to know that something is best under-stood as a hobby or a side hustle, not your day job.

I still love music. I work with a live band as part of my set. But music wasn't where my real talent lay. I still firmly believed that I belonged on those stages, but I wasn't sure I knew where.

I was a Black child of a single mother, living in the working-class South, a kid whose dad left before I was born, the product of a family whose poverty stretched back generations. We lived in my grand-mother's three-bedroom, one-bathroom home in a poor West Texas neighborhood with poor schools for poor people. By the time she was twenty-five, my mom had three children to care for alone. She worked so much that I can barely remember her being home. To top it off, she did it while disabled, having lost much of her eyesight in a work accident that happened when I was a small child.

But despite her odds, my mom never gave up. We barely had anything—but we had a roof over our heads, clothes to wear, food to eat, and plenty of laughter and love. Our life wasn't easy, but it wasn't terrible either. Matter of fact, one of my first jokes was that I didn't even realize we were poor until I was a teenager. When every-body is poor around you, nobody seems poor. You eat whatever's put in front of you. You go to school when it's time, and the rest of the time you spend in church. You don't sit around bemoaning your life and pouting about how poor you are—at least you didn't in my fam-ily's house. In our house, we ate pumpkin pie and watched *Star Search*. That was enough.

I came to realize that struggle has the potential to break you, yes, but struggle can also clarify goals and offer a sense of purpose. Strug-gle can motivate just as intensely as it can depress and infuriate. Struggle isn't necessarily aimless, even when unsuccessful. Struggle can help light a path, inspire ambition, and outline desire.

Inspiration came from other sources, too. Every time I'd go to the mall in El Paso, there was the reminder that I shared a name with one of the most famous brands in the world—*Frederick's of Hollywood*. So what if they sold lingerie? To me, that name was a symbol, a signpost for my future. Every time I saw that sign for *Frederick's of Hollywood*, my sense of destiny was reinforced. I was going to Tinseltown one day. I was meant to be great. And I believed that, down to my bones, my entire life.

But my mom wasn't just in my DNA. She was in my attitude, too. When I say I was a world-class mama's boy, know that we are talking the absolute worst kind. The ones you don't want your daughters to marry. I mean, Tyrese-in-*Baby-Boy*-level bad. Didn't want to leave my mother's side ever. Do you know that I didn't even go to Disneyland until I was in my mid-thirties because I was such a mama's boy? My brother used to travel with my grandma all the time. She took him to Disneyland, on cruises, to Las Vegas, all kinds of places. But I never went with them.

Apparently, from the way they'd tell me the story, I would always be like, "Is my mother going?" in this whiny, nasally, annoying voice. "Is my mother going?" And when they said no, I would be like, "I don't want to go." I was really bad with it. This is also a fact that they remind me of every time I see them for the entirety of my life. *Kev, you remember when you didn't want to go to Disneyland because your mom wasn't going?* Over and over and over, I'd be hit with this reminder. It got tiresome. "Yes, I remember. *OH, BROTHER. YES, I REMEMBER!*"

When you think about it, why would you let a *little kid* tell you he doesn't want to go to Disneyland? I think my family used to bait me so they could save money and be like, "Well, he *said* he didn't want to go." *Obviously, I want to go to Disneyland! I'm five! What do I know?!*

Of course, money *was* tight, especially when I was little. Our small home in El Paso housed nine people—plus a dog named Sunshine. (For the life of me, I don't know why nine people sharing three bedrooms would have a dog, but we did. And we gave the dog the same food we ate: collard greens, macaroni and cheese, all of that. He ended up having the same ailments, too, from hypertension to diabetes. The joke was that my great-grandma would take one blood pressure pill for herself and give another one to the dog.)

We were a close-knit, matriarchal family, with multiple generations crammed under that one roof. Of course, figuring out how to fit all those people was often a struggle for us.

Did I mention that that house had only *one* bathroom? Nine people plus one toilet equals a whole lot of awkward moments. Listen, I don't know if you know anything about old people, but they take a long time in the bathroom. And when one of those people is taking a lot of prescription medicine, their boo boo stinks! You want pain? Try being nine years old and walking into the bathroom after your great-grandma blew it up. *That* is pain.

We also had only one TV—which means you watch what your grandma watches. Oh, you want to watch *DuckTales*, little guy? Too bad. You're watching *Perry Mason, Matlock,* and "Victor Newman." And no, the show is *not* called *The Young and the Restless,* it's called "the stories" or "Victor Newman."

That we made it work was a testament to just how much we cared for each other and just how far we'd go to keep our family intact.

We were one of those Black households where everybody—children, grandkids, nieces, nephews—refers to Grandma as "Mom" without anyone ever being confused about who you're speaking to. My grandmother was firmly in charge, and we respected that. No matter how tight space was in that house, my grandmother always had her own bedroom—even though *her* own mother, my great-grandma, also was there. So forget the notion of nine people divvying up three bedrooms. What it really was, was eight of us trying to make do with the two bedrooms that were left. My great-grandma shared a room with my mom, my aunt, and, once she was born, my sister. My brother, my two uncles, and I all shared a bunk bed. I shared a bed with one uncle, Jay shared a bed with the other. They were barely in high school when I was a toddler, so we got along well enough.

Because the age gap between us was so narrow, we didn't refer to my mom's siblings as Uncle This or Aunt That. We just called them by their first names, which apparently bothered some people. (After my mom married my dad, I recall his people thinking it was highly disrespectful that we didn't use the Uncle or Aunt titles.) But that's just who we were as a family. We respected our young aunts and uncles. We just called them by their first names. I mean, how're you supposed to talk to a teenager who shares a bunk bed with you like they're some wise elder? We all up in here eating peanut butter sandwiches together and going to school, so everybody can just *relax*. How you my uncle, but you got football practice and homework?

My mom's marriage marked the biggest change in my early life. Up until she married my dad—William O. Kelly, the stepfather who raised me and my siblings—she essentially was a workaholic. She'd had Jason when she was sixteen, me when she was nineteen, and my sister at age twenty-three. None of our fathers were in the picture, and since she was the oldest of her siblings, along with taking care of her own children, she carried the responsibility of watching out for her brothers and sister, too. At one point, my mom had three jobs and three different uniforms. Most of my memories of her in that first house are of her coming home in one uniform, taking it off, and then putting another one on before going right back out the door. She had just enough time to change, grab a sandwich, and head out to her next job. I am pretty sure I got my work ethic from these moments. She was willing to do whatever. Most days she didn't even have time to take a shower. Come home in a Whataburger outfit, change into a gas station outfit, and go.

Then one day, she met the man she'd love for the rest of her life.

She didn't mean to. When I asked her about how she and my dad met—and if I'm honest, I never thought much about it before I started writing this book—she explained to me that she had been invited to a church anniversary service by her friend Nadine on the only Saturday she had off from work that month. Jason and I were off doing who-knows-what, so my mom had only my sister, Michelle, to look after.

My mom actually turned down the offer to go with her friend, but Nadine came by anyway, so my mom and my sister reluctantly went with her. To make matters worse, Nadine took my mom to a Church of God in Christ church called the House of Prayer. Most of y'all may not get why that matters, but for people like us—Christians who'd been raised devoutly in the Pentecostal Assemblies of the World movement—this was like crossing into enemy territory. COGIC vs. PAW? We're talking Hatfields vs. McCoys here. Yankees vs. Red Sox. Bad Boy vs. Death Row. The rivalry is real.

And that's when she first saw William. He was playing the drums in the church band. After service, my mom goes with her friend to the fellowship hall, and there he was again, getting ready to eat. They might never have spoken had Michelle not accidentally run into William and grabbed his leg. After a profuse apology, my mom sat with him and ate. Later they wound up talking on the phone. My mom initially thought he wanted to call her to complain about Michelle, but it turns out, after he realized that the woman with the clumsy little girl wasn't married, William wanted a date. Then another. Pretty soon, he was driving over from the base where he was stationed to take all of us out to McDonald's. Jason asked for the biggest burger they had, but we all wound up settling for Happy Meals. Not long after that, my mom got a husband, and my brother, sister, and I got the best dad anyone could ask for.

"The moral of the story," my mom said after she finished reminiscing about her love connection, "is that good things happen when you go to church!"

When my dad came in, he changed the trajectory of our lives. He was a military man, so after they married, my mom, my sister, my brother, and I wound up leaving our little house and moving into housing on Biggs Army Airfield, where he was stationed. He brought a stability I'd never known before. The moment we moved in with him, my mom stopped having to change uniforms. She was suddenly home all the time, free to do what she wanted—which was to create, to write, and to start businesses. I get my business hustle from her. But I want to provide for my family like him.

My life would've been totally different if they didn't get married, if I had stayed in El Paso my whole life or didn't leave until college. Without that man coming into our lives, there is a 1,000 percent chance I'd have had a baby out of wedlock and been working down at the plant. I don't know *which* plant, but I would have wound up working in it. My dad wasn't a rich man by any means. Our family still had our share of struggles even with him in the home. But those struggles were nothing like what our lives would've been without him.

Now, having said all those wonderful things, let me tell you how this same family cheated me!

You know what I never had that I always wanted? What both my siblings had that made their lives so much more enviable than mine growing up? What I utterly, shamefully, and inexcusably was robbed of as a child?

Godparents! Yes, you know that close family friend who you designate as an extrafamilial support system before your child is born? The one who stands with your parents at your christening, who augments all your birthdays and Christmases with those additional cards and $20 bills and knit sweaters? My siblings both hit the jackpot. My brother's godfather is an anesthesiologist at a hospital in El Paso, which is the only good job *in* El Paso. And his wife is a doctor of nursing and a professor. Those are his godparents. My sister, I think one of my grandma's friends was her godparent, but that's because she was the first girl. Everyone from Cinderella to the Corleone family had one, but not ya boy. Not little old ugly Kevin. Nooooo, he lived in a cage and survived on old, discarded biscuits.

I became aware of this unforgivable injustice as a small kid. My brother would brag to me all the time about how he was going to visit his godparents, how they were taking him out of town. And my sister, she would get showered with all these gifts from her godparents all the time. Me? Nada. So one year, I ask straight up: "Who are my godparents?"

My mom and dad were like, "Well, umm . . . God loves you! God is your parent. We weren't able to really find none specifically for you, but as you know, we're all children of God."

I was like, "Yeah, cool, I get that . . . *buuut* they're getting presents. They are getting *additional* presents. They are getting presents, *and* they also have God. I am not getting those. Who is the person to give me those?"

Yeah, I never got that answer.

I think they tried years later to find me godparents, but it was too late at that point. It never took. You can't just get godparents at thirty-four. I had bills by then.

As a kid, I was so jealous of my sister and brother that it drove me crazy. One day, I was unable to contain my envy of Michelle any longer. I'm forty-one, and I remember this so vividly that I'll never forget. We had just moved to our first duty station ever after living in El Paso: Fort Belvoir, in Alexandria, Virginia. My sister had just gotten a pink elephant for her birthday, a pink elephant with a white belly. I remember going into her room, where she had all these stuffed animals that she always got for her birthday. And I'm staring at this pink teddy elephant while I've got a glass of sweet tea in my hand. I'm burning a hole in this thing with my eyes because I'm so mad that Michelle got this. Suddenly, I just snapped. I ran up like some melodramatic reality TV star and threw my drink on the elephant! It landed right on the belly, the stain spreading like blood from a fresh wound. I was so happy and proud in that moment that I had ruined her elephant, that smug stuffed smile now covered in Lipton. *Take that, godparents' girl!*

The funny thing is, Michelle kept that stuffed animal forever— I'm talking about till she graduated high school. A week after the incident, I started to feel bad about it, but for years afterward, that elephant haunted my conscience. Eventually, almost a full ten years after Teagate, I snuck into her room and just stole the thing and threw it in the dumpster. My sister never even noticed. I thought it was gonna be something big, but she just totally forgot about it.

MOTHER WIT

When I talk about my family, people usually assume I'm the funniest in the bunch. Sorry to say, that's not the case. The funniest person in my family, by far, is my mom. I mean, everyone in my family *is* funny—but my mom, she has always been on a whole other level.

Take the last time my parents dropped by my house to visit. My mom and dad step into the kitchen and suddenly, my dog starts humping my mom's leg. I mean, he's going at it! Everybody's all up in arms, yelling at the dog to stop, trying to shoo him away. Meanwhile, my mom's just standing there, slightly grinning.

"It's okay," my demure, devoutly Christian mother says in a perfect deadpan. "I haven't been humped like this in a while. It's kind of nice."

"WHAT?!" shouts my dad.

It was hilarious.

Sometimes, I tease my mom, trying to get her riled up about something. And right on cue, she will take things a step too far.

Me: So, Mom, are you and Dad having sex tonight?

Her: Nope . . . but only because I'm on my period.

Ugh. Okay, Mom, you win. I'm out.

SWEARING SIBLINGS

I was raised in a strict religious household. I mean, *very* strict. Women couldn't wear makeup or pants or earrings. And this didn't just apply to church services. In our church a woman was expected to wear a skirt anytime she walked out of her house. It didn't matter where or when you were going. We'd be at church picnics in El Paso, roasting alive in one-hundred-degree weather, and the women still had to wear floor-length blue-jean skirts. Sports? Forget it: Do you have any idea how hard it is to play beach volleyball in a denim skirt? No. Fun. Swimming? Whenever we went to water parks, the teenage girls were required to wear full bathing suits covered up by full-length, gown-like T-shirts. (When I got older, I began to realize just how many of the rules were aimed at women.)

But here's one rule that was universal: None of us could go out to the movies. The theaters were considered "sin"—even though nobody ever explained why we were allowed to watch those same movies at home. It was like the theater buildings themselves were literally sinful, not whatever movie was playing. Honestly, though, this rule never really mattered much to us because we couldn't afford to go to the theater anyway. That bit of sin was a little too pricey for our budget—so we'd wait for those same movies to come out on VHS tape.

And that's pretty much how it'd play out in our home, with my siblings and me doing our level best to stay on the right side of a long list of rules designed to keep us from indulging in debaucheries like women wearing pants or any of us going to the movies or playing cards. Honestly, it could be exhausting at times.

One day, my little sister and I decided that we'd had enough of the rules. We decided we were going to go wild for once. We decided . . . to cuss.

As I remember it, the decision was more spontaneous than thought-out. It was a Sunday, and we were at home in between morning church service and evening church. The adults were in the house talking, which meant that my sister and I had at some point been sternly instructed to get out of grown folks' business. So we walked out onto the porch.

I looked over at her and suddenly blurted out, "F*ck you!"

She looked at me like she'd seen a ghost—and not the Holy one either. A regular ol' ghost, an apparition, a phantom. I watched as she let the profanity soak in. A twinge of anxiety gripped me as I tried to decipher what her response would be. Would she cry? Would she run in the house and tell on me? My heart began to pound. *She's* definitely *about to tell on me,* I thought. *I am about to get the beating of my life!*

Then, Grinch-like, a sinister smile curled across her lips. And she fired back.

"F*ck *you*! B*tch!!"

Oh ho! I thought, my anxiety vanishing in an instant. *She's cussing back—and she's even adding stuff!*

There was no way she could tell on me now, not without risking the same beating I'd have to endure. So I decided to cut loose.

"Shut up, you ugly b*tch!" I fired back.

With that, Michelle unleashed.

"You shut up, you big fathead a**, ugly f*cka. Motherf*cka."

"You're a motherf*cka!"

"You ugly motherf*cka! Tell on me. I don't give a sh*t. B*tch face, sh*t ugly."

Okay, now she's flying off the handle. These cuss words don't even make sense. Also, has she been secretly practicing? I mean, I just started this out of nowhere, but she's talking like she had this on her heart for some time now. Had to.

Then I just said, "Hell." And with that, we both burst into loud laughter.

For years after that, Michelle and I would occasionally look at each other and ask, "You wanna go outside and cuss?" And of course, the answer was always yes. Then she'd follow me out onto the porch, and we'd cuss till our hearts were satisfied. The sense of catharsis was amazing.

After that, we'd repent and go back in the house.

BULLY

Growing up, I fought a lot. Well, actually, it would be more accurate to say I *was* fought a lot—as in, I often got my butt kicked. Not that I was unwilling to stand up for myself. Sometimes, I didn't have a choice. For a child growing up poor in a house constantly filled with people, family clashes were inevitable. So, yes, I was accustomed to yelling at my little sister, Michelle, when she took my toys or arguing with my older brother, Jason, about who gets to watch TV. But even then, I wasn't good at physically fighting. Which meant that when it came to the inevitable scrapes with other kids in the neighborhood, I lost more than my fair share of fights. I lost almost *all* the shares of fights. If shares of fights were Apple stock, I would've made someone else a billionaire.

Now, before you start thinking I was walking outside and getting smacked around all over greater El Paso, let me tell you that you are correct. I got my butt handed to me a lot. But! Let me also make clear that most of those early beatdowns came at the hands of one kid, my first tormentor: a wide-bodied, NFL-fullback-built elementary monster known around school as Fat Tony.

In many ways, Tony was your typical bully, bigger than most of the other kids, with hands so large that he only needed one to hold both of my wrists together completely. I mean, come on: What fourth-grader has hands large enough to wrap one around both of another kid's wrists at the same time? This ain't me being fat-phobic, either. I was fat, too! But somehow, Tony was much fatter and a whole lot stronger. I was convinced that, somewhere along our brief academic journey, Fat Tony already had been left back at least a grade or two. At least. This was before the George W. Bush administration. Some children were, in fact, left behind. Apparently they were taking steroids while they were back there, too.

But what also made Tony different was that he seemed to like me . . . at times. He wasn't in my class (I honestly have no tangible proof he was in *any* class), but he'd wait around to walk home with me from school—and, of course, to beat me up. We'd walk home together every day, sometimes engrossed in conversation. We'd chat about the school day or the teachers we didn't like or other kids in the neighborhood. I'd crack a few jokes. *Yo' mama so fat if she sat on a quarter she could squeeze a booger out of George Washington's nose.* (That was the funniest joke I knew for like twelve years and I said it all the time.) *Yo' mama so fat she jumped and got STUCK!* (That was another that was a hoot. You know how funny something has to be to consider it a hoot?! Really funny.) *Yo' mama so fat she got baptized at Sea World. Yo' mama so fat she stepped on a scale, and it said "to be continued."* He'd laugh, and I'd find myself hoping that I'd finally been funny enough to win him over and avoid that day's beatdown.

Nope. He always remembered.

There we'd be, going on about the Teenage Mutant Ninja Turtles. I'd say Michelangelo was my favorite, and he'd say, "Naw, man, Leonardo is the best." Then I'd go to defend Michelangelo again, and he'd just be looking at me like, *Welp, it's time to get beat up.* And, somehow, I always knew that this look meant it was time to get beat up. I guess, technically the look can mean *let's fight*—but when you can't fight, the look means *It's time to get beat up*. Knowing what was next, I'd throw up my hands, crossed at the wrists, in the vain hope of guarding my grill. It didn't matter. Inevitably, Tony would snatch me up, clench my wrists in one of those thick hands of his, and punch me until he got bored. My life had become a *Tom and Jerry* episode on repeat. Remember when Tom had Spike chained up and he beat the brakes off him? It was *that* episode. But just that episode. No other episodes were available for me.

I never told anyone about it. Partly out of embarrassment, sure, but less that than to keep my mom and dad from smacking me around, too. Back in the day, parents didn't care so much that you got into a fight with one of your peers—only that you won. At bare minimum, you were expected to give it your best and fight back. Since I did neither, I decided to keep my run-ins with Fat Tony to myself. Who wants to get a beating for getting beaten? (Side note: What absolute twisted logic! Your kids lose a fight and instead of covering them in love, you decide to whoop them, too?)

After a while, though, Tony began to relent, if only slightly at first. I started to notice that the more I made him laugh, the shorter the lopsided fight would be. Then, one day, I broke through entirely, had him laughing so hard that he didn't even bother to pummel me. He punched me one good time, more out of habit or some weird sense of obligation than anything else—but I could tell that his heart wasn't in it. After all, how (or in Tony's case, how *long*) can someone take joy in beating up their very own personal comedian?

The following day, for the first time in what seemed like forever, Tony wasn't hanging around waiting for me. In fact, he never waited around to beat me up again. I can't remember the jokes I'd told, but whatever they were, they did the trick. I'd worn him down and found a funny bone underneath all that fat.

It was the first time being funny paid off for me. I realized that humor wasn't just a weapon. Used the right way, it could be a shield, too. It may have been worn and dented from Tony's fat fists, but it had worked in the end.

Now, I'd love to be able to end this story by saying that my torment was over permanently. But that ain't what happened. As much as I'd like the moral of the story to be about the unifying power of laughter or how jokes saved me, the truth is that Fat Tony really only stopped smacking me around because his dad, a military man like mine, got orders from the Army and their family relocated. I would love to tell a tale where nice guys always win or the bad guys inevitably lose. But the truth is sometimes the bullies just bully you until they move or you do. Life is not a Disney Channel movie. You don't always stand up to the bad guy one time and the whole school gets behind you. Sometimes in life, your bully just beats you up until their dad gets transferred. Sometimes, you learn to endure.

I didn't always have to depend on laughter, though. It's not like I was a complete failure with the fisticuffs. I got in some wins, too!

Okay, *two*. I won exactly *two* fights in my life. But you better believe they were decisive!

Once, not long after I'd vanquished Fat Tony with my wit (I mean, after he moved), I went at it with this kid named Rick. Rick was another neighborhood schoolmate who followed the same path I walked to and from school each day. Unlike Fat Tony, though, he was built more like a normal child my age. I can't remember exactly what set us off. I just remember we were walking home one day when, out of nowhere, as if the narrator from the Mortal Kombat video game had suddenly popped into our heads, Rick and I realized it was that time: *Fight!*

I squared up as before, but this time I knew better than to let Rick go for my wrists. Instead, before he could touch me, I kicked him dead in the balls. Stopped him cold. Then, when he doubled over, I delivered an uppercut that I'd seen used in *Mike Tyson's Punch-Out!!* You remember how you had to punch to beat King Hippo? You had to jump to the left and then you had to throw a flying uppercut. That's what I did. Do you know how silly you look as a child jumping into the air and spinning into an uppercut? Very. But that was my go-to move. The Little Mac spinning uppercut. I was the one doing the pummeling now.

As quickly as I'd kicked and hit Rick, I took off, sprinting all the way home. (Call it a . . . hit and run! *Ba dum tsss!*) Fortunately for me, Rick didn't have the persistence of Fat Tony. He never tried to fight me again.

My second spectacular victory came against a kid named Marquis. One day, we were in his yard playing when suddenly the horseplay turned to roughhousing. (There is a stark difference between horseplay and roughhousing. I don't have time to go into it now.) Pretty soon, it was time to throw hands. But unlike my previous bouts, this one came with a crowd—namely, Marquis's mama. As our tensions boiled over, his mom gazed on proudly from the doorway of the front porch, looking like the wife of some baron from an old TV Western who was so pleased to own all that land. She just knew she was gonna be gratified by watching her son beat me up.

I'm thinking she's going to come out at some point and separate us, send me home, chide him. You know, do what grown-ups are supposed to do when little boys get out of hand. Instead, just as we started to circle each other, she rushed onto the porch . . . and began calling for my head!

"Kick his *ss, Marquis!" she screamed. (Not that I'm cussing here. I'm just telling you what the boy's mother said.)

I couldn't show it, but I was taken aback. *What kind of mother is this?* I thought. *Why isn't this woman stopping this? She's supposed to be the adult here!* Seconds later, I went from puzzled to pissed off. Even though it wasn't meant for me, her encouragement provided all the motivation I needed. Kick *my* behind? The kid who'd made Fat Tony beat him up less and kicked Rick in the balls?! Me?! *You wish, Marquis's mama!*

I began channeling my inner Muhammad Ali, balling up my fists, jumping up and down, bouncing on the balls of my feet. Wasn't gonna be any desperate jokes this time. No swift scrotum kicks. This time, in Marquis's yard, with his mother's shrieks for blood ringing in my ears, I was going to win outright.

As Marquis and I circled each other, something about my sudden show of footwork caught him by surprise. He looked down to see what the heck I was doing. Bad decision. That gave me just the opening I needed. As soon as his eyes went to my shoelaces—*BAM!*—I caught Marquis with a straight right jab to the face. He stumbled.

I shot a quick glance over at his mom, who was staring in disbelief. More courage swelled in my chest. *Yeah. Uh huh.* I hit Marquis again. Then again. *Pop! Pop!* He clutched at his nose, which was gushing blood now. His mom started walking over. *Oh, nowww you want to step in and play peacemaker? Now you want to be a wholesome mother?! Nah.* I hit him one more time, a final spinning punch, and my opponent fell over. I'd won.

His mom was rushing toward us now, scowling. The one-woman crowd had turned ugly. True to form, I took off running, worried that Marquis's mother might try to jump me herself.

Heart pumping adrenaline and pride, I savored my knockout. No desperate jokes this time. No kick-and-run tactics. For the first time, I had won a fight straight up (*then* I had run away). And for the first time, I felt a new level of bravado. Things were about to be different, I vowed. There was a new Fat Tony on the block. I was the bully now. Fat Kev!

———

Walking to school the next morning, I found myself on the hunt for my next victim. I was determined to cement my status on the school-yard by knocking someone else out. I spotted this Asian kid, fat like me but also wearing glasses. I figured that since I'd never fought back when I was being bullied, this fat kid wouldn't either.

Oh, was I wrong! And it didn't take long for me to figure that out either.

In hindsight, I realize that I didn't even know how to bully some-one. I was downright bad at it. I didn't have a menacing stare. I couldn't recite any bone-chilling threats. I didn't even have any good insults to hurl at the boy. So I went with, "Hey, kid!"

He turned around, staring quietly.

"What are those, glasses??" I shouted. Because, well . . . he had on glasses. (I did mention that I was bad at this, right?)

Nevertheless, the insult seemed to make an impression. I had his full attention now. But I wanted to take things further. I was ready to get to some pummeling. So I pushed him on the shoulder. It was a light shove, barely enough to even make him move. In my mind, it certainly wasn't enough to earn me what came next.

For the slightest second, I saw his right leg twitch. Then, before anyone could even blink, there was a blur. Then . . .

What was it they said in *The Sopranos,* something about how the gun that kills you fires so quickly that you never hear it coming? That's how fast this kid kicked me in my face. My brain never got the chance to register that his foot was hurtling toward my head. There was no time to react, no time to brace myself. His foot slammed against my jaw, knocking me flat onto my back. I went down hard, like a tree after the last swing of the axe. I was on the ground before I even felt the pain.

When I finally did feel something, none of it was good. My head was throbbing. My vision was blurred. I dimly surmised that my head must've hit the asphalt. I was concussed for sure. (I'm sure the NFL would've cleared me to play, though.) As I continued to gather my senses, I looked around for the Asian kid with the phantom roundhouse. He was six blocks in the distance, calmly walking away. I was thankful that he'd decided not to press the matter.

That was it for my failed run as the neighborhood bully. Right then and there, I decided I didn't want to try to push people around anymore. I promised myself that I'd make more friends than enemies. Over my life, that approach has proven to be simpler, much more fun, and a lot easier on the jaw and the pride.

Just as important, I realized that simply because someone does something messed up to you doesn't mean you should do it to others. I got bullied, won two fights, and then decided to try my hand at bullying. That didn't work out for me. Unfortunately, people too often endure wrongdoing only to turn around and mistreat others when they get the opportunity. My short stint as a bully taught me that this wasn't the way to go, and that lesson plays out today in my career.

Take paying people, for instance. In Los Angeles, it's customary for promoters to either not pay comics or pay them very little. I'm talking like earning $40 for a ten-minute set. But when I started doing *Keep Your Distance,* a livestreamed comedy series during COVID, I decided to cover all travel and ground transportation, pay comedians $500, and give them a copy of their professionally recorded set. I could have easily paid the $40 or refused to give comics copies of their sets and fought to own their material. But that wasn't the right thing to do. It didn't matter whether it was "the way things were done." Some traditions are terrible and shouldn't be repeated, no matter how long they've been in place. Thanks to lessons I learned as a failed bully, I was able years later to pour more into my community and do it solely because it was the right thing to do.

More important, I didn't have to kick anybody in their balls, and nobody wanted to kick me in mine.

FREAKNIK

In 1996, when I was thirteen, I went to the infamous Freaknik. If you don't remember (or if you're one of the few who haven't seen the Hulu documentary), Freaknik was this huge annual outdoor festival in Atlanta that was very much on the raunchy side. As the name implies, it was one big freaky picnic—like Girls Gone Wild meets Mardi Gras—but with young, beautiful Black women who were thicker than racial tension.

Unsurprisingly, I'd never heard of Freaknik until my friend Jamahl came to me with the idea to go. He had a brother who lived in Atlanta and figured paying him a visit was as good an excuse as any to travel to the wildest party of the year. I was an innocent church kid going through puberty. Once Jamahl explained what went on, I couldn't wait to hit the road.

In the time it took to drive from El Paso to Atlanta, Young Kev was introduced to the greatness and beauty of the Black woman. Everywhere we went in the ATL, there were beautiful, scantily clad women flaunting their sexual liberation. I didn't even know what the word *twerking* meant—but I knew that I liked what I saw: fat butts majestically gyrating every which way!

For a kid who used to watch Cinemax through the blurry lines on the television, this was like having a premium account to debauchery. It was like being in the "Back That Thang Up" music video, only in real life. I could not have been happier. Especially as a kid from the church, I wasn't supposed to see these things. But I did see them. Oh yes, I did.

I remember we hopped a ride on a MARTA bus, and I felt as if this had to be what Sodom and Gomorrah were once like. Voluptuousness everywhere. As far as the eye could see on the MARTA. I probably had a hard penis for a week straight. I mean, I literally could not believe what God had done for me.

It did get a little crazy sometimes. One time we were in a particularly crowded area, and the police controlled the crowd by moving people on horseback. They just rammed horses into the crowd to move people around. A stallion to move stallions, I suppose. Nevertheless, in the course of one short weekend, I became a man. For that, I am forever grateful.

When I got home, I made sure to lie good to my parents. When they asked what I'd done in Atlanta, I said, "Well, revival, of course. A good old-fashioned revival. Boy, the Spirit moved, didn't it?" To be honest, my parents will probably find out what really happened at Freaknik when they read this page. I've never had the heart to tell them.

CRIPS FOR CHRIST

It's no secret that many musicians lead wild lives. What many people may not know, though, is that a church musician can live up to this stereotype just as much as your average rapper or rock star.

Church drummers, for example, are notorious for getting girls pregnant. All the musicians get the girls, but the drummers are the biggest stars. They are equivalent to the superstar who smashes his instruments on stage and then returns to his hotel and throws his TV through an upper-floor window. Somehow, the groupies love every moment. And that's what being a church drummer is like . . . if you are a good drummer. (Which I was not, so of course I didn't get any spoils.)

At my old church, one of the drummers there got a girl pregnant. Not long after, the *other* drummer got a girl pregnant. But as crazy as that seemed at the time, not even those indiscretions could hold up next to the drama brought on by our church organist. Now, Obi, *that* was one wild boy.

One day I was standing around after service, chopping it up in the church lobby as Black folks tend to do. Suddenly, Obi came busting through the door leading from the sanctuary and rushed over to where my group was standing. He was frantic.

"Some dudes from the club last night are on their way up here to jump me!" he said.

I—I'm sorry . . . What? I vaguely recognized the words he was speaking—but nothing about them made any sense.

Then, in what felt like mere seconds, our organist ran out the front door just as five cars screeched to a halt in front of our church. Suddenly, I and the others in my group found ourselves standing in the parking lot as nearly a dozen dudes wearing black Nike Air Force 1s start jumping out of the cars.

"Where's Obi?" they screamed. "Where's Obi?!"

So there we were, surrounded in our church parking lot, clad in the finest cheap suits that K&G Fashion Superstore could supply, our matching church shoes placing us at an even more severe disadvantage. We barely had time to think before the blows started raining. Out of nowhere, a ten-on-ten gang fight erupted only a few yards from where we'd just wrapped church service! And let me tell you, we'd had *good* church right before that fight. I'm talking about hand-clappin', foot-stompin' *church*. People at the altar were shouting, singing "Anointing fall on me, anointing fall on me, let the power of the Holy Ghost fall on me," crying and lifting our hands in praise. Now, no less than thirty minutes later, we were throwing them hands. God works in mysterious ways.

It was our attackers, a group of guys who all appeared to be under age twenty-five, versus the people from our church. The fight was fairer than you might think. Our pastor, for one, had grown up in the Cabrini-Green housing project in Chicago, and it only took a few seconds for his old 'hood instincts to kick in. Before we knew it, he had placed two of the young dudes in headlocks, one arm coiled around each of their necks. "Young man!" Pastor yelled as the two guys struggled vainly to break free. "Young man!"

Meanwhile, I'm caught in the thick of things, too. I spot one of my friends getting choked out, so I rush over and toss the guy off him. Gasping for breath, my friend turned to me and said, "I think I peed a little bit." All around us, ties and suit coats flapped in the wind as we punched and flailed and scrambled to get whatever traction we could out of our Stacy Adams dress shoes. Do you know how hard it is to fight in hard bottoms? Especially when your opponents have on basketball shoes? Sure, black Air Force 1s are more associated with violence and crime now than basketball, but technically they are designed to give you traction on the court.

We'd learn later that Obi, our organist, had started this whole mess. Apparently, he'd decided to sucker punch another church's organist at the club the night before. Why were two organists getting into a fight at the club? Your guess is as good as mine. Unfortunately, we didn't have the opportunity to ask any penetrating questions at the time, as we were too busy trying not to get stomped to death by ten pairs of Nike death sneakers.

Even crazier: Our opponents were musicians from other churches! We were supposed to be brothers in Christ. Why were we throwing wildly-off-the-mark haymakers at each other?

Part of why it took us a minute to recognize these guys was because, throughout the fight, they kept yelling out gang slogans. "It's on Crip here, nigga! Crip!" they shouted over and over. Needless to say, once we identified them, we were as confused about the gang talk as we were about why we were scrapping in the first place. *Crip?? Y'all niggas are musicians!* Church *musicians!*

I dunno. Maybe they moonlit as gangbangers. That's the thing about church boys. They come in all shapes and sizes. The Crips for Christ, though, definitely threw us for a loop.

Perhaps we should've been scared, but we were too busy being confused and frustrated with Obi for dragging us into a fight. Whatever beef he had with the other guy, they could've settled it one-on-one and preferably without throwing punches. But once we saw all those dudes climbing out of that car with their intentions already set, we didn't have time to scold Obi or set up a conflict resolution program. We had to get down right then and there. Sometimes, with friends, you gotta go to battle for them first and correct them after the smoke clears. Fortunately, the dudes we fought were church Crips, so they weren't as dangerous as, say, "regular" Crips. These dudes were diet Crips at best.

Contrary to what Mobb Deep says, there really are such things as halfway crooks.

WHERE HOOP DREAMS GO TO DIE

In high school my biggest ambition was to make it to the NBA. Naive kid that I was, I figured I had as good a chance as anyone. I was good enough to play AAU in middle school and high school in El Paso. By my sophomore year, I was nearing six feet tall and a solid starter in AAU. I also played JV in tenth grade and was slated to make the varsity team the following year. I knew the players, the coaches, the system, and how I'd fit in the team's rotation. I was all set for my high school breakout. Then my dad got transferred to Fort Lewis, an Army base about nine miles southwest of Tacoma, Washington.

After that, my hoop dreams had a nasty collision with reality.

In my eleventh-grade year, I didn't make the varsity team because there was a student named Reggie Williams who played in front of me. Dude was an amazing athlete. Reggie was 6'4" tall, weighed 220 pounds, ran a 4.5 40-yard dash and owned a 36-inch vertical. Years later, in 2004, Reggie would be drafted ninth overall as a wide receiver by the Jacksonville Jaguars. *This* was the dude who played my position on the basketball team in high school. On top of that, there was another guy close to Reggie's size who also played my position.

Me, I was barely pushing 5'11" back then.

So my coach took a look at me and gave it to me straight. "Listen," he said, "you can either play a lot on our JV team, or you can be on varsity and sit behind these two guys. Mind you, they're never coming out of the game."

I remember feeling a dent in my pride. And then came a feeling of overwhelming embarrassment. Then soon enough, resignation. There was nothing to gain in arguing with him, and probably even less to gain by suiting up for the varsity squad. I loved basketball. If I really wanted to play, my choice was clear.

"I'll play JV," I agreed.

So now I make the joke that I played JV all four years in high school.

Truth is, I had made a business decision (which, by the way, turned out to be the right call because, true to Coach's word, Reggie and the other dude never came out of the games). I took comfort in knowing that if I'd reclassified when I transferred in from Texas, I could've been held back in tenth grade and granted two extra years to play on varsity. A lot of kids do that nowadays, but that wasn't for me.

As it was, I had a good time on JV. I was an undersized hooper, but I made an impact. I started every game. I scored, rebounded, ran the fast break. I mean, I was *hooping*. Best of all, we won nearly all our games.

Honestly, I started every game for every basketball team I ever played on, from elementary to middle school to AAU. I was hooping—but nobody was in the gym to witness it. You know that philosophical question about whether a tree toppling in a forest makes a sound if no one is around to hear it? Well, trust me, when a JV player hoops in an empty gym, nobody hears that either. I was playing junior varsity behind an all-world athlete destined for a career in pro sports. The best I could do in that situation was wait for Reggie Williams to move on so I could get my shot. And when Reggie decided to not play basketball his senior year, my chance came. I didn't terrorize our high school league, no, but I made my way into games and contributed. And that meant my pro hoops dream was still alive, or so I told myself. I reminded myself that even Michael Jordan once got cut from his varsity team. I was gonna be like Mike and use failure as fuel that would propel me to the league.

After high school, my coach got me a tryout at some small college whose name I can't even remember. Although I'd planned to go to the University of Washington, Coach wanted to give me a shot at earning a sports scholarship somewhere. I can't even remember the actual name of the school. Let's just call it Pinehurst Valley College or whatever. That's not the name of the place, but it did have the word "pine" in it somewhere, so let's just call it that. A scrimmage against players from this small-college team would help me get a sense of where I stood as an NCAA prospect.

So yeah, I show up at the gym at Pinehurst Tech or whatever, me and another homeboy of mine who was about 6'3", 6'4". We show up, and the coach puts us out there to see what we can do. I'm figuring I can do this because I've guarded Reggie Williams, who's 6'4" and a specimen of an athlete. Their biggest guys, like the forwards and centers, were bigger than Reggie Williams, sure, but their smaller guys, the point and shooting guards, were *much* smaller. So, having checked an all-world athlete like Reggie during high school practices, I'm confident that I can stay with their smaller guys.

I start off guarding the point guard—and this white boy immediately starts cooking me! I mean, he was crossing me up, hitting threes in my face, stealing the ball from me. I can't stay in front of him. I can't keep up with him. He is literally shaking and spinning me every which way. I can't score. I can't do anything. Plus, he was freakishly strong. Like country 'Bama strong. *Fat Tony strong!* I couldn't believe it.

I'm like, *Okay, I can't do nothing with this white boy. He's really doing a disservice to me.*

For some insane reason, I decided I'd have better success guarding a bigger man, so, in a classic example of making a bad situation much worse, I switched to defend this 6'10" power forward. And this dude proceeds to dunk on me, play after play. His teammates just started throwing the ball in to the post. *Dunk. Dunk. Dunk.* He slapping the backboard. *Dunk. Dunk.* The college coach calls me out of the scrimmage. I sit down, take a deep breath, take my shoes off, and I'm like, *I think this is it for me for competitive basketball.*

The University of Washington had guys like Brandon Roy, Nate Robinson, and Will Conroy, dudes who played successfully in the NBA. I'm out here unable to guard even white people at Division II Pinehurst A&M or whatever. If I couldn't make it here, I wasn't going to make it at U-Dub. That meant no NBA either.

So in that moment, I called it a career when it came to hoops. I never felt bad about that. I fear regret more than I fear failure. I think more people would have success if they were at least confident and tried before giving up. If you try and fail, you're not worse for wear.

But you also owe it to yourself to be honest about where you stand. I'm not one of those guys who says stuff like, "I would've made it if my coach hadn't hated on me!" Nope. My high school coach was absolutely right to play me on JV my eleventh-grade year. And the coach at Pinehurst State or whatever was right to cut me from that team. Failure had shown me a harsh truth, and I immediately made my peace with it. The truth is, as much as I loved basketball, I wasn't good enough.

My righteous indignation at not making varsity in eleventh grade proved enough to keep me from quitting high school ball, but it didn't propel me anywhere except into a comedy career. Sometimes you ain't going to the NBA so you better figure out something else to do in life.

ROTC

Once I accepted that my jump shot was not earning me a full ride to school, I enrolled at the University of Washington and did what most other American kids do to get through school: I took out a loan to pay my tuition. Problem was, I didn't have any money to keep going. My bank account was tapped out. My parents were, too. Money got so scarce, in fact, that Melissa—then my girlfriend— took out a loan for me to stay in school. From high school on, my plan had always been to marry Lis (I may refer to her as Lis from time to time. I call her Melissa in this book because you don't know her like that yet) and start a family. But to do that, I needed to figure out how to stay in school long enough to get a degree and find a decent-paying career.

That's when I decided I'd join the Reserve Officers' Training Corps (ROTC). At the time, it made all the sense in the world. My dad was an Army man whose military service helped stabilize and transform our lives. After my mom and dad married, I grew up shuttling from one military base to another for more than a decade of my life. I'd also met Melissa on a military base, and her family was a lifelong military clan, too. I'd be a natural, I thought.

Admittedly, my understanding of the military was simplistic. As far as I knew, you got a job, and eventually, everybody got promoted. Some people got promoted higher than others, but everyone got promoted sooner or later. Also, you always had a place to live, and you never really got fired. People might get in trouble in the military, sure. Some people even went to jail—but they rarely got kicked *out* of the military. That was good enough for me!

More important, ROTC was the fastest route to paying off my student debt. The way it worked was, you get a scholarship that's going to pay for your college, and when you graduate, you're promoted to officer. That meant more authority, a fatter paycheck, and life in officers' quarters instead of enlisted housing. (Side note: If you've ever lived on a military base, you know that this last point is no small distinction. On the bases where I grew up, the officers' housing was always *much* nicer than the enlisted soldiers' residences. I'll never forget the first enlisted housing unit where we lived, at Biggs Army Airfield. Our house walls were made of cinder blocks. Not all the walls, but three-fourths of that house was made of cinder blocks. It was as if someone had thought to make regular brick houses but then ran out after doing the front. I hated those nasty cinder blocks. In the winter, they would stay cold all the time. No matter how high you turned up the heat, they'd be cold from the outside in. You couldn't get warm. And there wasn't any insulation either! The cinder block was your wall, and it was all that stood between you and outdoors.) So yeah, even though money has never been an obsession of mine, I was determined to get into school, earn those officer perks, and finish up with a sociology degree so I could become a social worker.

Interestingly, I'd gotten a lot of encouragement to join the military while I was in high school—but none of it came from my family. Instead, it was the military recruiters who'd descend on schools like mine (that's to say, schools that enroll a lot of poor and working-class Black kids) who were constantly urging us to sign up to serve. Most people don't know how intensely kids in inner-city schools and military schools get recruited. The Army and the Air Force recruiters will be at your high school during lunch, sitting at their booths and regaling you with stories about how the military changed their lives. They'd load us down with all kinds of brochures touting army life. They'd tell us over and over how much we could save for college by signing up. Apparently, this doesn't happen in wealthy schools, but it happened in all my high schools, even ones that were not on military bases. And it was effective. So many young people I knew really did view the military as their best option in life. It was like a guaranteed job to us (but, again, not a thing rich kids have to worry about).

Nobody outright discouraged me, but my family wasn't crazy about the decision. My dad, who had spent most of his adulthood in uniform, seemed particularly unenthusiastic. I remember him saying, "It's hard. You're going to be away from your family. They say, 'Army first. Family always'—but they make sure to say *Army first*. The military's going to use you. Just make sure you get out what you need as well."

I think my dad just wanted me to do what made sense for my life. When I look back on it, his most urgent advice wasn't about joining the service but, rather, which branch to avoid: "Stay away from the Army!" he warned. Matter of fact, both he and Melissa's father were like, "If you're going to go into the military, the Air Force is easier. They treat you better." I wasn't about to debate them on that. So, within a few days of talking with our families, I signed up for Air Force ROTC. What was supposed to happen next was a bachelor's degree, an officer's ranking, and a lifetime of Air Force benefits.

What really happened after that was, I sucked at being in the military.

I mean, I was terrible. I despised everything about it. I hated the rules, the uniforms, the time demands, everything. I can remember living in a dorm that was maybe a twenty-five-minute walk from the school football stadium. Once a week we had PT, physical training, that started at 6:00 A.M. at Husky Stadium. Mind you, this was in Seattle, so it was cold and wet all the time. Imagine you're in college, where 8:30 is an early class for most people, and you have to be at PT at 6:00 A.M. to work out. I was in pretty good shape at the time, so I didn't mind exercising or playing basketball, but I hated to be up that early. I was staying up late a lot back then, till 1 or 2 in the morning. I'd be hanging out, eating pizza, all that type stuff. I would have to leave at 5:30 to walk thirty minutes in the rain (I was too broke for a bike or a car) to get to Husky Stadium for PT.

I probably was the most unmotivated PT person in the history of Air Force ROTC. When I joined, my commanding officer asked if I was in good physical shape. I answered that I played basketball three, four times a week.

"Okay," he said, "but are you in military shape?"

I said I was. I was not. Military shape is running and doing push-ups, sit-ups, and pull-ups. None of those things were required to play basketball. And I sucked at all four. I remember running the mile and thinking that there's no way a person did this in less than four minutes or whatever the Olympic record was at the time. HOW?! How could they do that when my lungs were on fire? Push-ups? My arms were weak. Sit-ups? Every time, I felt like I was gonna doo doo on myself. Pull-ups? Forget about it. I don't think I've ever done one successful pull-up in my entire life.

In the end, I was like, *Bro, I'm not doing this! This is stupid.*

What made it even worse was that on Thursdays, you had to wear the uniform. And I loathed that Air Force uniform, mainly because it had a stupid hat. It was one of those old-school 1950s drive-in-movie hats. The In-N-Out Burger hat. Fridays through Wednesdays, I'm wearing FUBU and spending all this money on whatever's popping: Nike, Adidas, all that stuff. And then I'd see my friends on Thursdays, and it'd be a whole different conversation.

Them: What you wearing *this* for?

Me: I'm in the Air Force.

Them: *What,* nigga? You in the *fake* Air Force?? You ain't in the Air Force for real!

Me: Nah, but I'm gon' be.

Them: So why are you wearing the uniform if you *gon'* be?

Me: Bro, you got to wear it once a week to be in the program.

You know how Black people are. Right away, my friends start going in: "This nigga's in the *fake Air Force!* This nigga can't fly no planes!"

After a couple of conversations like that, I was like, *Bro, I'm not wearing this!* It got to the point where I would wear the uniform in my Air Force ROTC class, but then I would hurry to my dorm and take it off.

Later in the day on Thursdays, we had inspection. You would have to wear your uniform. You'd have to spit shine your shoes. You'd have to iron your clothes, have your little In-N-Out Burger hat all perfect. You'd have to have your medals all lined up (which wasn't an issue for me since I had none), along with your name tag (which I did have).

Then they'd quiz you about the airplanes. They'd show you pictures of all the models, and you'd have to identify which was which. There were maybe six to ten fighter planes, then six to ten hauling planes. I remember, I only knew two planes, just their names. I knew an F-16 and a C-118 Globemaster . . .

. . . Uh, wait, lemme double check that . . . Nope, no, it was the C-17 Globemaster III . . .

See, this is what I mean! And those were the two planes whose names I recalled myself committing to memory . . .

Anyway, those two, the F-16 and the C-17, were the only two I kinda knew, so if they showed me a fighter plane, I would say, "F-16!" And they'd be like, "No, Raptor," or "F-18," whatever they are. I can't even tell you what the other ones are to this day. And whatever the cargo planes were, I would get that wrong, too. So I would fail inspection after inspection. On top of that, I would skip ROTC training and then get caught on campus later that day out of uniform. All these things were demerits.

As humiliating as all that was, however, what really made me decide to stop doing ROTC was when I found out how the scholarships were set up. Don't forget, I was putting up with all this only to pay for school. But then I found out something nobody had bothered to tell me when I was being asked to sign up: The scholarships are only for the kids who are in the pilot program!

Of all the jobs I thought I might do in the Air Force, flying the actual planes was *never* on that list. Even if I'd wanted to (which I decidedly did not), I'd never be a military pilot. My vision wasn't great. At six feet, I was too tall to fit in a fighter plane cockpit. And a brother had bad feet. The only reason I was doing this in the first place was to pay for school, make sure Melissa would be squared away, and avoid that cinder block housing. Once that realization about the Air Force hit me—*Nigga, I'm going through all this, and you're not even going to pay for my college?*—I immediately stopped caring. I already was doing the barest minimum to stay in the program. Suffice it to say that I did even less once I was clear about how the scholarship worked.

It wasn't long before I got called into someone's office and was told that I was being kicked out of ROTC.

I'm paraphrasing here, but the conversation was very to-the-point:

"Kevin, you're not really built for the military like that. You don't listen. You're not engaged. You're always out of uniform. You have a number of unexcused absences from PT. You've never passed an inspection even once. Sometimes, your shoes aren't even tied."

Honestly, they had me red-handed. I knew I didn't want to be in the Air Force. They knew I didn't want to be there. And *I* knew they knew I didn't want to be there. You'd have thought I'd take the dismissal as a welcome relief.

Instead, I sat in the office and cried. "No, man," I pleaded. "I need this. I'm going to live here. We're going to *do* this. I'll be good. I'll learn the planes." But none of that helped. I was done. The military kid whose family had spent a lifetime bouncing from one base to the next had officially washed out of officer training.

My dad was cool about it. As I said earlier, he really didn't want me enlisting. He respected the military and what it had done for his family, but he didn't want his kids to put themselves at risk of killing or being killed. He wasn't proud that I didn't make it, but I'm certain he was relieved.

Surprisingly, there wasn't much fallout at the university either. Basically, the officers in charge just went off on me, told me I was a terrible recruit, and demanded that I return my uniform. I'd figured the tongue-lashing was coming, but the request for my uniform threw me. Not only had I pretty much stopped wearing my uniform (because, again, I had no idea they could kick you out), I'd actively neglected it. As much as I would have loved to hand the uniform in and be done with ROTC completely, I couldn't even find all the pieces. I did have that stupid sock-hop hat, which I couldn't have been happier to turn in. Now, why did I march in there and return one loose Air Force hat? Because I hated that hat and I never wanted to see it again. I never did find all the other pieces, though, so the ROTC program threatened to charge me $500 if I didn't turn in the uniform.

Since I didn't want them to be mad at me but also didn't have

$500 to burn, I handled it in the most logical manner I could think of: I just stopped showing up at the ROTC building. I never went back again. They threatened to put a hold on my transcripts but nothing ever happened. The moment I stopped going to that building, I never even so much as bumped into the military people again.

But I'd learned a valuable lesson: You can't choose options just because they're safe or because they're choices your parents made. You have to do what's best for you. I'm actually quite thankful to ROTC for kicking me out. I wasn't cut out for the military ever, but honestly, if they hadn't kicked me out, I probably would've stuck with it and enlisted. Back then, I valued consistency above everything. But just because it's something consistent doesn't mean it's good or right for you. The goals you set should be yours, should reflect your true desires and ambitions. No, you're not going to achieve everything you set out to do, but you should at least know for sure that you truly want whatever it is that you pursue.

Plus, look at me. Overweight and slow. Do you think I am in a position to protect our country? Do you think enemies foreign or domestic would fear a man with plantar fasciitis?! I assure you, they would not.

SPARKS

If the early part of my life was spent trying on different roles—basketball recruit, military officer in training, schoolyard bully—only to have them blow up in my face, the following stages would be characterized by having a fairly clear sense of what I wanted to achieve. (And then having *that* blow up in my face, too.)

Around the time I was seventeen, realizing that I wouldn't amount to much as a drummer or bassist or a singer in church, I started harboring this crazy idea for another type of stage performance. The church talent show was coming up. I decided that I'd get up in front of that audience and do something that I'd never done in public before and that nobody had dared to even attempt at a Church of God in Christ function: I was going to do stand-up comedy.

I figured out as a kid that I was funny—and, more important, that being funny had its perks. I knew that if I could make my family laugh and keep them laughing, I'd get to stay up late and hang around grown folks. The same way I had used humor to disarm Fat

Tony, I used it to get in good with adults when they were usually sending the kids off to bed. The idea of being funny intrigued me. I loved the fact that just my words could make people laugh. I loved that I could tell a story and truly captivate people. Laughter is an involuntary response. You have to *make* people laugh. I loved that I could.

It wasn't until my early teens that I felt any true enthusiasm for actual comedy, though. Even then, it would be years before I burned with any real passion for the work I do today. But the sparks were being lit.

The first spark flared when I was about fourteen. That's when I fell in love with stand-up comedy, thanks to the routine of Jonathan Slocumb, a Christian comic who had just released a comedy album called *Laugh Yo' Self 2 Life!* I used to spend a lot of time with my dad in the car back then, and he always played that album. I probably could quote it word for word.

Slocumb had a joke about shouting music. He said, "You know that song 'You know you make me wanna shout'? Well, that song doesn't make you want to shout." He then had the band play real Black church shouting music. He then went on to say, Imagine if that song came on in other moments. Like when Tiger Woods hit the winning shot at the Masters. Boom! The music comes on. Or when you go to the grocery store and you only have $20 to spend and you HONGRY—not hungry but HONGRY. They ring your groceries up, and it's $19.99 and the shouting music comes on.

This was genius to me. He took something that was Black church–relevant, like shouting music, and applied it to a thing that everybody could relate to, like Tiger Woods winning the Masters or being hungry and broke. I saw clearly a way that I could take my experiences in church and get everybody to laugh, church people and anybody who's ever bought groceries. The blueprint was laid. And I intended to follow it.

It wasn't only Jonathan's routine that fascinated me, but also his stage: He was doing real stand-up comedy *in church*. Who knew? Certainly not me! As I've explained, I grew up in very traditional, very strict congregations. To say that comedy was not a thing when it came to our service is an understatement. You have the devotion. You have praise team. You have the choir. Anything that veers from that is viewed with deep suspicion. For instance, when the K&K Mime Ministry, a pair of brothers who use mime to share the gospel, first came out, the people at my church had a problem with that. When the gospel duo Mary Mary released their smash hit "Shackles," people at my church complained that the song didn't mention Jesus directly.

They say "praise you," not "praise Jesus." Why can't they say "Jesus"?

They're playing that music in the club. How you gonna worship God, and they're playing that same song in the club?

My church was the type of church that got mad at Kirk Franklin for releasing "Stomp" because they felt like the song was too reminiscent of hip hop. It sounded like "the world" to them, so they did not want people to listen to one of the most prominent and beloved gospel artists of our generation. And when it came to actual secular music, forget it. I grew up not even knowing who Anita Baker was.

But you know what I observed about those same church folk? At the same time these people were wagging fingers at Mary Mary and warning of the dangers of Kirk Franklin, I also noticed that when I'd make fun of, say, Sister Daniels's style of singing or how the pastor preached, they would all dissolve into laughter and giggles. They might complain about church music that seemed too steeped in secular society, but they had no problem laughing at jokes drawn from our shared experiences as Black Christians. Why they would get mad at one thing while laughing at the other confused me, yes, but I'd also confirmed that humor was effective. And thanks to *Laugh Yo' Self 2 Life!*, I knew that same approach might actually work on a larger scale, even if I never imagined that I'd be the one trying it.

The next bolt of inspiration struck three years later, when I took Melissa out for a movie on what would be our third date ever. (The "no movie" rule had relaxed by then.) Our first date was to see the movie *Gladiator*. On our second date, we saw *The Fast and the Furious*. For our third date, we went to see *The Original Kings of Comedy*. Now, like most Black teenagers, I had seen *Comic View* on BET and *Def Comedy Jam* on HBO. I knew who Steve Harvey, D. L. Hughley, Cedric the Entertainer, and Bernie Mac were, of course. But never had I imagined that a stand-up comedy show would resonate so powerfully on the big screen. There was something about watching those performers in a sold-out movie theater that felt much bigger than watching them in our house in front of our little TV. I also don't think I ever laughed as hard in my life as I did at that movie. That was my second spark.

So I'm seventeen, looking for my niche in a family full of talented performers. Burning with a newfound love for comedy, I hit on this crazy idea to try a stand-up routine in front of a church crowd that could be as humorless as they can be judgmental. If I succeeded, I'd have broken all-new ground. If I failed? Oh, the reprimand would probably be epic. I was still on the fence about trying when I mentioned my idea to my brother, Jason. Jay had always been supportive—he'd wind up helping me on the business end of my career—but I think he might've sensed my hesitance about trying something so offbeat for our congregation. So right away, he tells me how this girl in our church didn't think I was funny and that she would be rooting for me to bomb.

I was mortally offended! Not funny? She might as well have walked up to me, taken off one glove and slapped me across my face with it. The gauntlet had been thrown down. The challenge had been issued. Up till now, I was only kicking around the stand-up idea in my head. But now that I knew I had a hater in the crowd, I was determined to get up there and prove that she didn't know what she was talking about. Chip heavy on my shoulder, I entered the talent show immediately. We were about to see about all that "not funny" business.

And no lie, I went out there and killed that day! I talked about getting whoopings as a kid and how parents would pause with every hit. *Didn't* *smack* *I* *smack* *tell* *smack* *you* . . . I'm telling you, these people were dying! That same crowd that could be so crusty when it came to Mary Mary and mimes was bursting into loud laughter at nearly every joke. I don't think I was up there more than five minutes, but everything I touched on was something they could identify with as part of their own Christian experience. For my closer, I told a joke about how preachers sound like they're having an asthma attack during their sermons, stretching out each syllable while drawing deep, loud breaths between each phrase.

"Anddddd . . . uhhhh . . . I'm tellin' you, saintssss . . . uhhh . . ."

When I finished, everyone was cracking up and applauding. A deep sense of satisfaction filled me as I stood there and let the ovation wash over me. The claps and cheers were all the affirmation I needed. Where was that hater now?! Surely, the girl who'd claimed I wasn't funny was going to change her tune now.

I don't think I saw the girl after that show, but I did run into her years later. And when I bumped into her, I just had to ask her about what my brother claimed she'd said. (You'd think I would've forgotten about it by then, but nope. I was still a little salty.) Thing was, she had no idea what I was talking about. She'd always found me funny, she said. Here I had been holding this little grudge for all these years, and she had no clue that I felt that way or had any kind of a problem. Jason had lied.

When I finally asked my brother about it, he admitted that he'd made up the stuff about her not finding me funny—but he did it, he said, because he didn't think I was really planning to go through with the comedy routine at the talent show. He was throwing a battery in my back to get me all excited and make sure I followed through. And sure enough, that's exactly what I'd done. That was Jason for you. He knew me. More important, my brother believed in me even when he worried that I didn't believe in myself.

DOO DOO

In my senior year in college, I doo dooed on myself. I realized just now, in this moment, that I've never written this down. The word *doo dooed* just looks hilarious. I could use *pooped* or *dookied,* but I just feel like *doo dooed* fits perfectly what happened.

Now, had I been drunk or doing some outrageous stunt, maybe then it'd have been understandable. Most people figure that when you're in college, you get drunk at some point, and in your drunken stupor, you pee all over yourself thinking you're in a dream . . . or worse. One too many passes of the Courvoisier, a few too many Incredible Hulks, and anything can happen, right? What do kids drink in college anyway? I'm only referencing things I've heard in rap songs. Maybe Everclear. Anyway, that's a drunk story that you might even be proud to share on some level. At worst, people can relate because "we were all crazy in college."

Not me. I can't claim to have been partying. I wasn't passed out. I wasn't drunk. Matter of fact, I didn't have my first drink until I was twenty-nine. The one college party I went to had fewer than three people there when I arrived, and I immediately felt like the rapture was gonna come, so I left. It wasn't nothing but pride that led to this whole fiasco.

The story starts simple enough, with Lis and our shared love for rocky road ice cream.

Back then, Melissa and I used to ride the bus from Seattle to Tacoma on Fridays to see our family and friends back home. She would stay with her parents; I would be at my apartment. Every Friday after our last class, we'd meet up at her dorm room to chill until it was time to catch the bus that ran straight to the Tacoma Dome Station. Well, on this particular Friday, I spied a pint of Ben & Jerry's Phish Food ice cream, my favorite, sitting on a table in her dorm room. Although we both loved ice cream, she was not a fan of Phish Food; she said it was too much. But to me, Phish Food was just right. Instead of just chocolate ice cream, marshmallows, and almonds, Phish Food had little chocolate goldfish and caramel drizzle. Phish Food was a sign that God was real and he loved me.

So, I asked her if I could have it. And that's when she tried to warn me. The ice cream had been sitting out all night, she said. It was warm, she said. If I ate it, it was certain to tear my stomach up, and, since we were about to be on a forty-five-minute bus ride, she said she didn't think that would be an ideal time for my stomach to be all messed up. All rock-solid advice. Fantastic points made all around.

But one of my problems is that I was always determined to prove myself to her, even to my own detriment. I wanted that ice cream to prove to Melissa that she was wrong about me, to prove that I was a real man—with an iron stomach! I was gonna show her that.

"I can handle it," I said.

"Kev, you're gonna mess up your stomach," she told me.

"Lis . . . I said I can handle it," I repeated, even more determination in my voice.

"Ohhkayy."

I didn't know it at the time, but that "okay" didn't mean "I believe you can handle it." That "okay" really meant "Go on and do what you gon' do. You'll learn your lesson soon enough." (It was early in my relationship with Melissa, so I didn't know the difference.)

I picked up the pint and as soon as I put the spoon into it I knew it was going to be a problem. The spoon cut through the ice cream like a hot knife through warm butter. If I was a wise man I would have been like, "You know what Lis, you probably right. This *is* gonna mess up my stomach." But I was not a wise man. I aggressively stuffed the ice cream in my mouth and pretended it was HITTING! It was not. It was not at all. It was warm, just like she said, and disgusting. But that wasn't the point anymore. As a real man, I felt obligated to prove that day-old warm ice cream was no match for a stomach made of steel.

Pretty soon, it was time for us to catch the bus. The stop wasn't even a ten-minute walk from Melissa's dorm room, but one minute in, I knew I was in trouble. Every step I took made me feel like Calvin Rodgers was playing his world-class "Rain on Us" drum solo in my intestines.

As a real man, I didn't want Melissa to have any idea that she was right. But she knew. For every five steps forward I took, I was forced to take one step back. Air leaked out of my body with relentless aggression. I. WAS. IN. PAIN.

And Melissa took joy in all of it.

She kept asking if I was okay. "Yes," I lied as I motioned for her to keep walking. After what seemed like hours, we finally made it to the bus stop. We probably had another fifteen minutes to wait for the bus. There was a Subway at the bus stop, and Melissa suggested I go in there to poop. "There might be traffic and if there is you won't be able to make it," she explained.

More solid advice. I knew she was right—but the real man in me was in too deep. I had to see it through, my boy! Plus, that Subway bathroom was locked, and the key was attached to a long serving spoon. You know what that means. Disgusting bathroom. Anytime a place has the bathroom key attached to a long object, the bathroom is guaranteed to be absolutely disgusting. I sit on public toilet seats, but it has to be the right situation. A nice hotel lobby, Nordstrom, the Delta Sky Club. But not Subway.

"I'll make it," I told her.

"Ohhkayy."

That was the second "okay" in the same hour. I really should have listened.

The bus arrived. Within minutes, we were on the freeway. Traffic was clear for as far as the eye could see. I was relieved. Forty minutes to Tacoma. I could do it. Then, just as we neared the Seneca Street exit in downtown Seattle, the freeway became a sea of red brake lights. It wasn't even rush hour yet.

"Oh no," I said to myself. I mean, it was out loud, but I was talking to me.

"You okay?" Melissa asked.

I nodded sternly. "I'm good."

I was not good. That was a lie, a lie from the pits of hell.

"Okay," Melissa said. "I'm gonna take a nap."

A nap? I thought. *You're just gonna go to sleep and leave me to the consequences of my own actions? Let me lay in the bed I made?! How selfish!*

Five minutes later, she was sound asleep.

Meanwhile, I was fighting for my life.

The temperature inside the bus shot up two hundred degrees. My stomach boiled like a witch's cauldron. I tried to stand. Didn't help. I sat back down. Didn't help. I'm not saying I started to cry—but let's just say that tears formed in my eyes. And they fell.

After twenty-seven minutes, I seriously contemplated pooping in my backpack. I mean, I actually opened it, looked inside, took out my notebooks, and sat them on the seat. I was long beyond caring about the other passengers seeing me. That wasn't what deterred me.

It was the backpack itself. It was this really nice JanSport model, and I didn't have money for a new one. So I held on. For forty-five minutes. Then an hour. Then an hour and fifteen minutes. Finally, we neared the exit for the Tacoma Dome. *Six red lights to go. I can do this.*

I could not do this. It was like my body saw the exit sign and decided, *Welp, that's close enough!* I was holding it. I promise I was. But then my booty hole just gave up. I was still holding it—but it could no longer be held. I clenched—but the clench wasn't clenching like it used to clench before. First, a little poot escaped. Then the poop moved closer to the exit.

"No, no, no, no," I whispered to myself.

Too late. My body surrendered, bit by bit. My sphincter betrayed me. Your sphincter is supposed to keep your booty closed when you need your booty closed. It held me down for as long as a sphincter could, but then it felt like it just gave up the ghost. Finished its shift for the day and was ready to go home. A little poop dribbled out. I couldn't believe it, and what's worse, I couldn't stop it. I never stopped clenching my booty, but my booty stopped being clenched. Next thing I knew, I was full-on pooping. I was still holding it, but it no longer mattered. Poop was coming out of my body. I was broken, dejected, a shell of a man. I pooped all in my draws. Melissa woke up and immediately started laughing. I sat in silent humiliation—and poop—through the six red lights.

When the bus finally stopped, I stood up. Some of the poop went down my leg and got caught in my pants. Thankfully, I was wearing windbreakers that cinched at the bottom, and that little taper caught the poop. I sauntered off the bus and into the bathroom. I tossed my underwear in the trash, cleaned myself up as best I could, and we went to my apartment.

Here's the thing, though. All that summer, I told the story at barbecues and church. My friends and family used to fall out laughing. They would beg me to tell it again and again, no matter how many times they had heard it. It became my first real closer in stand-up. It was hilarious and true. I worked the angle about relationships and pointed out that if you just listen when your girl says "Ohhkayy," it will keep you out of trouble. Men and women reveled in that. I pointed out how stupid it was to try to prove to her I had an iron stomach. I could have just listened. It brought them into the story, and it always set me apart from other comedians. It was very different than what other comics would say on any given night. Most comics wanted to be funny but also wanted to remain cool. To be honest, most comics, at least male ones, are trying to be funny, trying to get paid, and trying to get some coochie as well. Me? I wanted to be funny and memorable, and that was it. I knew those stories would hit and would set me apart. And since I didn't want no coochie, I could feel free to be as honest with my jokes as I wanted to be. In comedy, there's nothing that you can't use as material if you aren't afraid of it.

I still have the same style of comedy today: Take something very truthful about me and try and make people relate. And if they can't, at least make it funny so they laugh. There is a YouTube video of this story on my old kfred926 YouTube page. As I write this book it has 403 views. Posted on October 21, 2009.

But there was a life lesson, too, a very messy one, to be gained from the whole ordeal. I learned that there is literally no value to be gained from going against someone who just wants to help you. Melissa was not my enemy. She had nothing to prove to me. She knew me well and knew how this would go. Pride and ego left me with dookie around my ankles. There was no reason to have dookie around my ankles.

PART TWO

Finding Funny

BOMBING: PART I

By the time I was in college, I didn't need my brother to manufacture critics for me. I started running into plenty of real ones on my own. Throughout my time at U-Dub, I would take these little gigs at parties and small eateries, the occasional church function. And that's where I found out quickly that not everybody thought I was funny. In fact, there were plenty of times when I was certain nobody would ever laugh at my jokes again. I bombed a lot in college.

The first time was at this fraternity step show. You know step shows: They're those big gatherings of Black Greek-letter fraternities and sororities like Kappa Alpha Psi, Omega Psi Phi, and Delta Sigma Theta, where the members perform elaborate syncopated dances. Think movies like *Stomp the Yard*.

For whatever reason, I was asked to host the event. Problem is, I'm not Greek. Personally, I think only members of Greek-letter groups should host Greek events. You can get away with stuff if you're in the organization that you can't get away with if you're not a member. (I could explain what jokes you *can* get away with if you are not Greek, but since I am not Greek, I would be stepping into dangerous territory. If you know a Greek person, you can for sure ask them. Not me. I am just a humble servant of the Lord.)

I was familiar enough with them, though, to understand the gravity of my circumstances: If I screwed up at this step show, I'd have scores of angry Black college kids in Greek-letter paraphernalia calling for my head. I was nervous. Worse, I wasn't prepared. This was my first gig, and I made the mistake of thinking the crowd was there to see me. In fact, they were there to see a step show. They were there to stroll around showing off their dance moves and to have a good time. Not one person had come out to see a new comedian mess up. And, man, did I mess up.

My first mistake was that I got on the mic and stopped them from strolling so I could start the show. They immediately had an attitude. I didn't even do a good joke to quiet them down. I was just like, "All right, all right! Enough of that! Listen to my jokes!" It only made matters worse that the jokes I told weren't worth the *shhhh*.

Then, when time came to start the step show, I committed the cardinal sin.

"Give it up," I shouted, "for the brothers of Alpha Kappa Alphaaaa!"

Alpha Kappa Alpha is a sorority. I'd meant to announce Alpha Phi Alpha, a fraternity. I had studied this on index cards all month, but bombing early in the show had shaken me. Now not only had I offended two powerful and proud organizations, I'd offended them both at once. What hit me the next few seconds was like a shotgun loaded full of boos. *Chk chk BOOOOOOOOOOOOO.*

I didn't try another joke all night. And I haven't performed at a step show in the fifteen years since. Won't. Sometimes you gotta know when you have no business in other people's business.

BOMBING: PART II

Another embarrassing moment was the time, in college again, where I did a set at this coffee shop. Bombed the whole way through. This was back when my big closer was telling people about the time I doo dooed on myself. So I sit on the stool and start acting this thing out. I draw my face in tightly, eyes clenched, nose wrinkled, as I rock back and forth to show them how hard I was trying to keep my bowels from betraying me. I channel every desperate, pathetic, hilarious moment I could recall from that humiliating day on that bus to Tacoma.

And nobody's laughing.

Then a few minutes later, I go to sit on the stool again and the stool breaks. I tumble to the ground. The mic hits the floor, and all you can hear is feedback. *Znnnnnnnnnn!* I just got up and left. My confidence was shredded.

I quit comedy for six months after that.

Somewhere along the way, I wound up taking another gig. I can't recall what specifically got me back on the stage, but I know that I loved comedy so much that I just didn't want to go out on a loss. I did great, too. The doo doo joke made a big, um, splash this go 'round.

Sometimes you don't need big wins. The small victories can be enough to keep you going. But I'd be lying if I didn't admit that those early defeats hurt.

THE NATE JACKSON
SUPER FUNNY COMEDY SHOW

By the time I graduated U-Dub, I was knee-deep in real life and responsibilities. Melissa and I were married in 2004, during my junior year in college, and we now had a place in Tacoma. I owned a mountain of student loan debt. We'd welcomed the birth of our first son, Isaiah, with Josiah soon to follow. Even though I was still dabbling in comedy, I was tired of working venues that weren't even really venues. Being funny had its perks as a kid, even into my late teens, but as an adult, making old-fashioned church deacons and stoic ushers laugh didn't pay our bills or clothe our kids. I performed intermittently, but mainly my life centered on church, family, and work.

In my last few months of college, my career trajectory was altered suddenly and dramatically. For much of my time at the University of Washington, I had planned to become a social worker. I chose sociology as a major because, one, I didn't want a degree that I had to take a math class to earn (I absolutely *hated* math) and, two, I loved people, and sociology is the study of people. Problem was, I didn't find out until I'd chosen my major that there really aren't jobs in sociology that don't involve being, y'know, an *actual sociologist*. I wasn't interested in the research. I wanted to work with people—kids, to be specific. When I brought this problem to one of my counselors, he suggested I get into social work because that's where the money was.

I was all set to follow his advice . . . until I spoke to an actual social worker during one of my classes. He explained to me that there wasn't any real money in social work either, not unless I planned to go back to school for a master's degree. *That* most certainly wasn't happening. Melissa had already taken out one loan for me. And I had run up so many loans of my own that I was pretty sure the bank would lock the doors in my face if I showed up asking for more. Now this guy was telling me I'd have to run up more debt just to have a chance to pay off the debt I'd already accumulated? It was too late to consider switching majors. I realized that I had washed out yet again, this time before I'd even had a chance to start. The best I could do, I told myself, was hope that I'd find a job, any kind of good-paying job, that required some sort of college degree.

Thankfully, I landed a gig in the banking industry not long after graduation. It wasn't really calculated, just sort of happened. At that point, I wasn't sure where I was headed professionally. Making a living mattered more than chasing any career dreams. So I applied for and landed a position in personal banking at Bank of America in Tacoma. As it turned out, I was good at it. I can't say that I was fulfilled—Melissa always knew I wasn't the type who liked working for anyone else—but I was meeting my obligations as a dad and a husband, and that was good enough. For the next five years, I pretty much was resigned to filing comedy away as a long-lost dream.

Somehow, though, comedy managed to find me again. When it did, that fading dream soon started to become realer than I ever could've imagined.

One day at B of A, I struck up a random conversation with one of my personal banking clients. She was a kind, older Black woman whom I had started working for not long after I got my job. I can't recall what we talked about, but I usually kept it light and humorous whenever I was handling a client's business. As it happened, she thought I was funny—so funny, in fact, that she handed me her son's business card and urged me to give him a call.

"My son is Nate Jackson," she said as she handed me the card, which was decorated with a large image of her son's smiling face. "You should meet him. He has a comedy room in Tacoma that he runs on Thursdays."

In the years since, Nate Jackson has become a roaring success in comedy, thanks in part to TikTok and in larger part to his skill. Back then, though, Nate was only beginning to make a name for himself, running his comedy show on the second floor of a local restaurant. The place had an event space that the owners wanted to get more out of, and Nate had convinced them to turn this event space into a comedy club. Every Thursday, they would come in and build the stage, bring in the instruments. They had a huge bar. He worked out a deal that allowed him to keep proceeds from the ticket sales and a portion of the bar.

Nate was an amazing businessman. Because the Black population in Tacoma is so small, he was able to market to everyone in his immediate demographic pretty easily, and he was brilliant at it. He had reached out to all the Black kids who grew up in Tacoma and to the military families who'd settled there. His pitch was straightforward: If you grew up in Tacoma, you already knew there was absolutely nothing to do there. But his Thursday night shows, he said, were gonna change all that. Nate's shows sweetened the pot by offering audiences two nightlife experiences in one. He was giving you the comedy *and* the club in the same place, at the same time. Sure, the other six nights in Tacoma may have been as boring as folding pants. But on Thursdays, Nate was going to give you something to look forward to.

His program was called the Nate Jackson Super Funny Comedy Show, and for those of us in Tacoma, it was the biggest thing ever. Now, thanks to my chance meeting with his mother at my job, I saw an opportunity to go from watching Nate's show to being a part of it.

But I was wary. I hadn't told a joke to a crowd since bombing at the coffee shop, but something in me was still desperate to try. I knew I was a funny dude. This nice lady with the comedian son had affirmed as much. But doing an entire routine at a real comedy showcase? In front of a strange secular audience? For free? I had kids to raise and a wife to keep happy. I had a mortgage, light bills, car insurance. Nothing about it seemed sensible, or even convenient, at that time. And yet, for days, I couldn't get his mom's suggestion out of my head. Nate Jackson was my age. We had graduated college around the same time, maybe a year apart. Fast forward five years, and here I was working a desk job at some tired bank while he's out there really doing stand-up comedy and being successful.

It didn't take long for me to arrive at a sobering realization: *Nate Jackson was living my dream.*

A few days after getting Nate's card from his mom, I was at Albertsons grocery store picking up fried chicken for dinner after work and decided to give Nate a call. (By the way, for those who don't know, Albertsons's grocery store fried chicken is amazing! I stand by that! I'd rather eat there than most fried chicken places. And me and my wife order from there *often*!) I'm standing there waiting for my chicken, talking to Nate about his show, and unexpectedly, he offered me a spot in the lineup.

"Yeah, man, you want to do comedy?" he asked. "Come up and I'll give you some time."

Just like that, I had booked my first gig.

That would be the final spark that enflamed my love for comedy—and lit the earliest steps of my path toward actual success. Until then, my most memorable moments with comedy were as a fan. Jonathan Slocumb had shown me that a Christian-themed brand of comedy was possible. *Def Comedy Jam* and *Comic View* had introduced me to a new wave of Black comics and stand-up styles that I love to this day. And *The Kings of Comedy* taught me that comedians can be larger than life. But Nate Jackson had given me a chance that showed me that comedy was truly possible for a regular guy like me.

I can't remember exactly what my set was. I jumped at the opportunity so fast that it seems like a blur now. I just remember that when that first Thursday came, Nate called my name and urged me to go up on that stage and rock out for as long as I want. And I did just that. From there, for the next two and a half, three years, every single Thursday, you could find me on the second floor of that little restaurant holding forth for twenty, thirty minutes at a time at the Nate Jackson Super Funny Comedy Show.

This wasn't LA or New York, so I had no idea that this wasn't traditionally how it's done. In the bigger markets, even outside of New York and Los Angeles, comedians have to go out and find open mic nights. Each night, up-and-coming comics migrate from bar to bar, club to club, and add their names to long lists of would-be performers in hopes of getting short stints under the bright lights. You'll get onstage at some small venue with only ten or fifteen people in the crowd, and you do the best three minutes of stand-up that you've got. Then you move along and hope that the person who performs next doesn't make the sparse crowd forget about you completely.

That wasn't how I began, though. I was fortunate enough to start my career at the most popping comedy room in Tacoma. Nate's room packed in as many as three hundred people each week. (It was notorious for attracting a bunch of 'hood niggas as much as anyone else from Tacoma.) Half of the room would be people mingling in the back of the spot—and paying no attention whatsoever to the performer onstage—because the bar was located back there. The front hundred and fifty, they mostly were there for the show. But almost everyone who came out was also there because they knew that after Nate's show, the venue turned into a nightclub. It could be difficult to get and keep the audience's attention some nights, because people would be in there pregaming, and I remember some comedians getting deeply frustrated because so much of the crowd ignored them.

But I never had that problem. Whenever Nate or I went on, people would immediately start paying attention. If you were killing, the hundred and fifty people in the back would be listening. If you were not, they were not. And that's how I learned to hit the stage with energy, to grab their attention right away. I didn't know how to structure a set back then, but I knew how to play to the crowd's energy. Nate had a DJ and a live band, which made the show much more interesting. No other comedian used the band, because most comedians don't use music. But I always got the band involved. I would come on requesting that they hit me with an R&B song or some kind of backup music. The band members were mostly church musicians playing at the club trying to make a little extra cash. That's the atmosphere in which my stage persona was crafted. Even when I first started doing tours, my sets always came with a live band. I'd have the live band playing during my set, interspersing my jokes with the music, slowly building up to the funniest jokes in my set, which, of course, I saved for last.

At Nate's, I was able to hone my routines and find my voice as a comic. I wasn't the guy to go onstage with a cigarette and stand there for a half hour making quiet observations. I reveled in the energy and up-tempo pace that was the hallmark of Nate's shows. My comedy style drew on all those years sitting in pews, taking in the showmanship of the preacher and choir director, all the charisma of the

Black church. I acted like a preacher, even when I "preached" about a current hip hop song. I had the musicians play R&B chords behind me as I turned gospel tunes into R&B jams. Sometimes I feel like the call-and-response that happens in the Black church is ingrained in us. So when the band picked it up, so did the people.

I'd never performed anywhere larger than a church auditorium before I got to Nate's, but overnight he enabled me to rock sold-out crowds and do routines that were nearly as long as some comedians' Netflix and HBO specials today.

That said, I'm sure a Netflix special paid more than I was earning from Nate. Because I wasn't earning a penny, not at first anyway. Don't think that I'm complaining about this, because I'm not. Not at all. I was a total unknown with no experience, so what Nate offered me was just as valuable, and that was opportunity. He gave me the chance to not only dream about success but to prove week in and week out that one day, I was going to be a great comedian. Fridays through Wednesdays, I would bask in the ambiance of my earlier sets and spend increasingly more time working on how to top my own act. I was holding down my B of A job—at least for a while— but the effort I was putting into my comedy was growing right alongside my deep desire to get better at it. And each Thursday, I would see that effort pay off.

All week long, I was Kevin Fredericks, working stiff and loving father and husband. Come Thursday at Nate's, though, I could say *I'm a comic.* You'd find me running up to the mic at that little restaurant announcing myself energetically in front of hundreds of other Tacoma partygoers: "What's up, everybody, it's Kev on stage!"

BECOMING KevOnStage

So about the stage name.

It is what it is at this point—KevOnStage—but if I'd have known back then that I might really become a success as a comic, I promise you I'd have put a lot more thought into what I want to be known as. At the time, it was meant less to be my stage alias than a pseudonym to keep me from getting fired from the bank. Social media was taking off big back then, and it was the era when almost everybody used their real names online, especially if they were trying to promote themselves. I was a big social media user from the beginning, and on Facebook I used my real name, Kevin Fredericks. But then Twitter started to grow, so I hopped over there, too, and started to pick up an even larger following.

Twitter in those days was the Wild West. People were posting all kinds of stuff. And it wasn't long before I noticed that some of them were getting in trouble in real life for reckless comments and antics online. It was easy to get to them, too, because in a lot of cases these people had their first and last names all over their accounts. Anybody could, and in many cases would, google posters' names, discover where they worked, and email those people's bosses to rat them out, hoping to get them canned. Naturally, this worried me because I was talking as crazy as anybody, making all kinds of wild jokes. (I would love to add some specific examples here, but those jokes have been erased from my mind—and my timeline—for my safety and career.) It was only a matter of time, I fretted, before some dude I'd roasted on social media attempted to get me back. And I could *not* afford to lose my bank job! So I decided to switch it up.

The brainstorm session went something like this:

I'm Kev . . . umm . . . I be onstage . . . All done!

No kidding, that is all the consideration I gave it. With that, I started changing my name across social media. It went from "Follow me @Kevin Fredericks" to "Follow me @KevOnStage." And soon, that's what audiences began to know me as when I performed. I'm good with the name now, of course, but if I had it to do again, I probably would go with something a little flashier or maybe something funny.

Instead, I now have people who think my first name is Kevon and my last name is Stage. It's ridiculous.

NIGGA DADDY

I've already told you how one of the most unfortunate incidents of my college years—me doo doo-ing on myself on the bus—turned into my first truly great stand-up joke. The second was based in truth, too, but also was the result of some creative embellishment. It was a joke I used to do called "Nigga Daddy." It was a hilarious bit that audiences loved. I had to retire it, though. I'll explain.

Early on, my wife and I lived in a mixed-income neighborhood called Salishan. It used to be super 'hood, but developers tore down the government housing and replaced it with beautiful single homes for sale and rent. Since the homes were pretty cheap, we had purchased one. Nice little crib, but the area was still 'hood. For example, one night a group of Samoan Bloods jumped a recruit in my front yard. It was something like 3 A.M. I heard commotion outside, and when I looked out the window, I saw all these dudes punching and kicking some kid into my family's Honda Civic.

My wife: Go out there and stop them!

Me: Stop Samoans from beating up their friend?

That's the kind of neighborhood it was. Heavy gang activity. 'Hood mentality in nice houses. Kendrick Lamar's *good kid, m.A.A.d. city*—but in Tacoma.

When my oldest son, who's a really sweet young man, was getting ready to attend a school in the neighborhood, my fear was that he'd have to adopt a tough mentality to make it. And that's how the joke was born.

I set it up with my son going to school in Salishan and me worried about him getting involved in gang activity on day one. Crowds immediately got the joke. They knew Salishan was the 'hood. They knew Black people were the Crips and Samoans were the Bloods.

I'd say, "I'm afraid he's gonna come home after his first day of school and be like (in a heavy Crip voice), 'Wassup, nigga daddy?!'" The crowds would die laughing.

And then I would say, "What did you call me?"

"Nigga daddy . . . 'cuz you my nigga and you also my daddy."

Roars of laughter.

"Well, what did you learn in school today?"

"A is for apple, B is for ball, and C is for cuzzzzzzz!"

When I got to "C is for cuz" (*cuz,* short for *cousin,* is Crip slang for fellow Crips), the audiences would be banging on the tables. Then I would just go down the alphabet and use all the letters, but replace them with gang/drug related stuff. D is for drugs, E is for *ese* (a Mexican gang term), F is for felony, G is for G-Unit.

This joke was an absolute monster early in my career. I did it *all* the time. If I didn't do it, regulars would scream out, "Do Nigga Daddy!" So I would. But then I started finding myself in places like the grocery store and people would yell out, "Wassup, nigga daddy!"

At the mall: "Wassup, nigga daddy!" At church: "Wassup, nigga daddy!" (At least at church they respected the house of God enough to whisper the joke.)

After a while, I realized that I had to retire the joke, even though it was a killer. First off, my wife and I had moved into better jobs, the kind where your boss doesn't want to see videos of you doing a bit like that. Also, my son had grown older, and it felt kinda disingenuous to keep telling that joke as if he was still in grade school. Most important, as funny as the joke was, I realized that I couldn't have people just walking up and calling me a nigga in public.

Some of y'all want to lean into that phrase a little *too* hard.

BOMBING: PART III

I t's wild how success can set you up for failure. During my time working Nate's shows, I was a big hit. No matter how raucous the crowds, I was always able to go on stage and give a commanding performance. My name was starting to circulate locally. People were even coming out expressly to see my sets. Even though I'd never done anything larger than the gigs that Nate organized each Thursday, I had come to believe that I was more than ready to step outside that comfort zone. I didn't realize then how much I still had to learn.

I found out the hard way one year when I entered a well-known comedy contest in Oakland, the Bay Area Black Comedy Competition. The competition, which was run by a guy named Tony Spires, had been around since the 1980s. It's the venue where a bunch of greats got their start. Jamie Foxx blew up there. Chris Tucker, Lunelle, Nick Cannon, D. C. Curry, Mike Epps, Katt Williams— these are some of the competition alumni. I think Nate Jackson won it the year before I entered. So now here I was following in Nate's footsteps. I wanted to be a star, too!

Melissa and I traveled to Oakland together. It cost me three hundred bucks to enter. And the whole time, I'm thinking I'm going to kill it. In my mind, I was envisioning how my big break was going to unfold right there in Oakland: *They're gonna be like, "Brother, you got it!" I want you to move to Hollywood right now. We'll figure out how to get your family down here, but you need to be on set Monday morning!*

Meanwhile, little do I realize that everybody who's there is good. I don't even know most of the comedians at that point. But I'm crushing it in Tacoma, so conquering Oakland shouldn't be much different. *I'm going to kill this so bad that I'll probably quit my job after my first set!* I'm not even joking. This is how good I just know I'm about to do.

My confidence was doubly boosted on the first day of the competition. That Thursday, before the real judging even began, the comics were given a chance to warm up at an open mic at this small room in Oakland. The big sets began on Friday and ran through the semifinals on Saturday and the finals on Sunday, so this was just a chance for people to get a little practice in before the real showcases.

I didn't know any of the names, but five comics in a row bombed that first night! I mean, nobody was alive. The crowd was sizable, but very few people were laughing. Every comic who went up there and failed came backstage to complain about the audience.

"It's the crowd, man," someone said. "The crowd is weak."

Someone else told me, "You're going to take the same L we took."

In my head, though, I'm like, *I'm not about to take no Ls.*

And then I went out there and had a great set! I got the crowd back. My friend Lance Woods goes after me, and he has a great set. And then the next three or four guys go, and they all have great sets, too. So I'm not worried about the crowd. In my head, I'm already measuring myself for the comedy competition crown. *I'm going from Oakland to Hollywood!*

The next night was the first night of the competition. It was held at Yoshi's, a popular jazz club and restaurant in Oakland. Each comic was given three and a half minutes to get through his or her set. Right away, I was thrown off. I'd never done three minutes before. I was used to going up onstage at Nate's and taking my time, fooling around with the band, using each joke to build to my final, show-stopping crescendo. The night before, I'd spent about ten minutes working the crowd. Now I was going to have to condense my set.

I opened up by being honest with the audience.

"I've never done three minutes before," I confessed. "I hope I do good. If I don't, I don't got enough money to leave so I'll just live here, on my mama."

Not funny. Nooobody laughed. Apparently, that's a very common, very hack-y joke that hundreds of comedians have done over the years. A lot of that audience comes to the Bay Area competition every year; they've heard that joke way too many times. And I'd made it worse by adding the phrase "on my mama," which was Oakland slang. I heard audience members clear their throats.

Now I'm starting to panic. I'm thirty seconds into my set, and I'm not sure if the three minutes that I have left are too little time or too much. I tell another joke that gets a little bit of a chuckle, but I am painfully aware that I'm not doing well. Another joke, slight chuckles. Then I decide to try out this bit where I spoof an R&B performance, taking a gospel song and singing it like it some super-steamy soul ballad. I'd first developed the bit at Nate's, where I had access to the full band and where it comes toward the end of a twenty-five-minute set where I've already got the audience thinking I was funny. I hadn't planned on doing the joke in Oakland, but I was desperate. I was falling flat on my face in front of the audience, my peers, and whatever agents and talent scouts happened to be there searching for the next Jamie Foxx. So I launch into the joke, singing whatever gospel song I'd decided to use as if it was a Jodeci hit. I'm rolling my body, pouring water all over my chest, all of that. I used to be killing it in Tacoma with this joke! I needed it to go over as big now as it ever had at Nate's.

No one laughed. At some point, I locked eyes with this woman in the front row and saw her tilt her head back away from me in disgust as she tried to make sure none of my water dripped on her. For some reason, I remember the water feeling frigid. The water was always cold when I did this joke, but I had always been rocking before and sweating heavily, so it always felt refreshing. Now, with all these un-smiling people staring at me, that water was freezing. I'd spilled it all over the stage. And people were glaring at me like, *What is this nigga doing?*

On the biggest stage I'd ever performed on, I was having perhaps the worst performance of my life. *Not only am I not moving to LA,* I thought, *I'm not moving forward an inch in this competition.*

I walked out of Yoshi's with my shirt over my head and shoulders. I didn't even think about where I was going. I just headed straight away from the club as fast as I could, hoping nobody spotted me. I must've walked for a mile before I stopped. I didn't even text my wife to let her know where I was going.

I didn't go back to see the rest of the competition. I didn't even bother to find out who won. I was so hurt, so shaken to the core, that I did something that I hadn't even considered since I started performing at Nate's: I quit comedy.

PUTTING IT BACK TOGETHER

For the next nine months, I was consumed with dejection and aimlessness, at least where comedy was concerned. Oh sure, I had a decent, albeit dull, job at the bank, at least for a while. But my faith in myself was shot. Watching a dream go up in smoke so humiliatingly in Oakland had left me unwilling, almost afraid, to even try to crack another joke. I couldn't bring myself to go anywhere near a venue. No Nate's. No church shows. No open mics. No cafés. Kev was officially off stage, probably forever.

But in time, my retirement really became more of a reevaluation. I knew deep down that I still longed to stand in front of an audience and make them laugh, but I also had to give serious consideration to the type of comic I wanted to be. I wasn't cut out for those quick-hit stand-up sets that young comedians all over the country cut their teeth on. Maybe it represented a flaw in my ability, but nine months away from comedy had forced me to accept that I had certain limitations. That's why, to this day, I have never entered another comedy competition again.

What I did do, though, was focus more intently on the one thing I knew that I did do well: long-form humor. I was great at extended jokes and skits. I was awesome with a live band. I knew how to move the crowd. It just took me longer to get cooking, that's all. I also realized that my love for longer-form humor fit perfectly into the ever-expanding social media landscape. I began to step up my online presence, posting more jokes and skits on YouTube and Facebook. And I still did short sets; they just weren't the heart of my routine.

Believe it or not, only a few years later, I ended up back at the Bay Area Black Comedy Competition—this time as a panelist in a symposium about using social media to build a comedy brand. Not only that, but I also was living in LA by then, chasing that same Hollywood dream I once thought I'd blown up forever when I bombed at Yoshi's.

It was freeing to return to the scene of the crime knowing that I hadn't allowed that setback to stop me. Did I perform? God, no! But I had grown so much as a content creator and social media influencer that people were no longer evaluating me by someone else's rubric.

I learned back then that I have a profound knack for pivoting whenever I'm confronted with an adverse situation, that I can whip up some lemonade from the sourest of lemons. That, as much as anything, has enabled me to recover from my worst bombs.

And hey, all it took for me to embrace that was getting run off the stage in my first and only comedy competition.

PLAYMAKERS

Comedy may have been my first love—and the inspiration for any number of failures I endured—but it wasn't my sole entertainment passion. It wasn't even the first thing that I invested in that flopped horribly. Back in the early 2000s, when I was a rookie still trying to find my niche in entertainment, I didn't only do comedy sets. I also wrote plays that I hoped one day would be performed on theater stages around the country. I'd seen guys like Tyler Perry become hugely successful doing Christian-themed plays for Black audiences—plays that they would film and sell on DVD following the stage performances. Perhaps my destiny lay there, too.

Back then, Tyler was going platinum in the 'hood. Even God-fearing church folks had no problem buying bootleg versions of his plays. The fact that the material was pirated—or to be more direct, *stolen*—didn't deter pastors, first ladies, deacons, and church mothers from buying and watching it. Tyler was relatively clean, but he sometimes cussed, and the church folks ate it right up. Long before I ever actually watched one of Tyler's plays, I was introduced to them by someone constantly quoting his scripts. I wanted people to talk about me like that and to quote my plays, too.

That was the genesis of Playmakers, the church-focused YouTube series I used to do with my brother back in the early 2010s. Back when we were doing those stage plays, you couldn't have told me that I didn't have the next Madea on my hands!

I put everything I had into those productions. I ran up something like $10,000 on my credit card trying to build that business, writing and producing the plays, finding venues for them, and filming them for DVD. Problem was, we didn't have any strategy. We were just doing things. For instance, we went out and spent $500 on a debit machine to handle business transactions, because we thought we'd be out on the road selling all this merchandise related to our plays.

On top of that, we spent $5,000 on building a set. We paid for studio time to record songs for the plays. Once, we paid a sound engineer to record the audio for our play only to realize the dude was eating a burger and having a cigarette when the play started. He missed the first thirty-seven minutes. Yeah, he apologized, but by then it was too late! We'd had only one night and one show to nail the play, and we didn't because this audio engineer just assumed that we wouldn't start on time! And yeah, maybe his assumptions were well-founded, given that plays rarely do start on time—but we weren't paying him for his assumptions. We wound up having to bring the actors back in so we could dub their voices—which meant we had to pay the cast all over again. Talk about a disaster.

Additionally, I got the bright idea of trying to go directly to major producers and investors to get them to sink cash into our projects. I figured that if I could just get one DVD into the right producer's hands, he'd immediately fall in love with my work and want to underwrite everything. So I decided one day to take a gamble and fly from Tacoma to Miami to attend an expensive fundraiser that featured Je'Caryous Johnson, the playwright and author best known for adapting stage plays from books like Eric Jerome Dickey's *Friends and Lovers* and from movies like *Two Can Play That Game* and *Set It Off.* Once Je'Caryous got a chance to read my work, I was sure I'd be in line for an adaptation, too.

Of course my wife, being the practical and realistic person she is, was, shall we say, hesitant about my gambit. Walking up to a famous playwright unannounced and shoving a DVD into his hand somehow didn't strike her as a well-thought-out stratagem. "There is no business plan here, Kevin," Melissa told me frankly. "This isn't a plan at all. At best, it's an interaction."

But I wasn't listening. In my mind, the plan was as airtight as any scheme out of *Ocean's Eleven.* So I spent $6,000 to go to the fundraiser, which included a $500-a-plate dinner. I remember walking up to him and shaking his hand, steeling myself for the exact moment when I'd hand him the DVD of our play and ask him to consider backing us.

"Yo, Je'Caryous, nice to meet you!" I said eagerly.

"Nice to meet you, too," he replied politely.

He shook my hand. Then he walked on by and never said another word to us. Didn't even take a DVD. Because what else was he supposed to do? He had no idea who we were or why we were shoving things into his hand. He had no meeting on the books with us. He probably was on his way to the bathroom or something. It was in that moment that I realized just how stupid "the plan" was. Nobody's going to put you on just because you walk up and start talking. I should've listened to my wife.

Instead, I continued to burn through money with outlandishly unrealistic investments. Once, I paid something like $3,000 to attend an acting class sponsored by actress Tasha Smith. I'd met her out somewhere and, as a matter of courtesy, she had invited me to attend her class if I ever found myself in New York. And course, I'm fronting like, "Oh yeah, I'm in New York all the time!" So we bought some tickets and took the class in hopes of getting closer to Tasha. Afterward, we go up to her and were like, "Tasha, can you put us on?"

"You're already on," she said. Then she left.

That was a $3,000 lesson, one that our small business couldn't afford. It took us six or seven years to pay off that credit card bill. Actually, we didn't get it paid off completely until Tracey Edmonds, the TV producer, gave us $50,000 to make ten episodes of a YouTube show. Until then, we just paid the minimum on that credit card every month for years, and the balance never went down.

Another time, I was determined to meet gospel music impresario Fred Hammond. My Playmakers collaborators and I found out where Fred lived, and we went to his house! We put a DVD on his front door with our business card, thinking that that would put us one step closer to being discovered. Nothing came of it. Fred (who I know well now) doesn't even remember getting our package. Again, why would he?

As costly as those lessons were, they were strangely effective. I learned that spending money aimlessly doesn't build a business. It just builds credit card debt. That's not how you approach it. If I'd pitched Je'Caryous or Fred beforehand, if I'd reached out and tried to set up a real meeting, I might've had more success. But I was so hell-bent on making it that I didn't bother to think things through. In some ways, I haven't changed. I've never been afraid to talk to people or to sell myself, and there's a reckless hope that you sometimes need in entertainment. Whatever I am going to do, I go full force ahead with it. If I have a show idea, I can still go from idea to execution quickly.

But I've learned to think through the realistic steps I can take to achieve my goals. Now I'll make a call or talk with an acquaintance before trying to just walk out and meet someone. I'll brainstorm. I'll seek wise counsel from friends and family. This isn't to find excuses not to execute, mind you. I don't want to be on my deathbed saying I wish I would've tried something, so I try everything. But learning to set myself up to actually succeed—that took some time to learn.

DREAMS DON'T DIE

Even before the comedy competitions and DVD schemes, I had apparel dreams. If I wasn't going to hit it big as a playwright, basketball player, or musician, I would make my fortune selling clothing and related merchandise under my own brand. I called it Dreams Don't Die. And just like with my plays, I went all out. Forked over top dollar to a designer to come up with some Dreams Don't Die shirts. Paid for models and photo shoots. Put together a couple of Dreams Don't Die commercials. Even did voiceovers for the spots. We spent about $15,000 on the shirts, along with about $5,000 on everything else.

We wound up selling like $712 worth of shirts. Then we ended up having to knock the price down to like $2 a shirt just to get rid of the rest of our inventory. Ultimately, we wound up giving them away.

Dreams don't die.

Well, they do if the shirts don't sell.

BANK FRAUD

I never wanted to work for other people. One of the biggest reasons I couldn't quit comedy permanently, even after bombing in coffee shops and at step shows and in Oakland, was because, deep down, I always hoped it would become my path to self-employment. Even after the disaster in California, I'd decided to go back to Nate's because I loathed the idea of spending the rest of my life tied to a desk with a supervisor perched on my shoulder.

Unfortunately for me, that's what my life had become following college. Stuck with a sociology degree that I was no longer planning to use, I spent my weekdays at Bank of America opening checking and savings accounts for housewives and grandmothers in greater Tacoma. Ironically, as much as I would come to hate working in banking, you should know that when I was locked in, I was amazing at my job. We were located near a huge military population and had a large Spanish-speaking community as well, so the stream of traffic into the bank was constant. My co-workers figured I would need

help for a long time, which meant they would have to table their
own work to get me up to speed. But what they didn't know was that
because I had grown up in El Paso, even my limited Spanish was
more advanced than anything they knew. This meant I could ask all
the questions necessary to open an account when they couldn't.

Que es su dirección?

Donde es su trabajo?

Cuanto dolares para deposito?

Firma aquí.

My Spanish was bad, but my Spanish accent was awesome! I
might have struggled with the words, but my enthusiasm for speaking Spanish to our customers was unmistakable. They appreciated
the effort, too, and that resulted in my colleagues' diverting more
potential customers to me.

Being from a military family gave me another advantage, given
our proximity to the large military community in the area. Having
grown up with an Army dad, I understood their needs in ways that
many of my other colleagues couldn't imagine. I knew they worried
about being able to transfer money online while they were deployed.
Online banking wasn't as easy then as it is now. Cash App and Zelle
didn't exist. To transfer money from one bank to another meant
going into a branch and paying $15 for a wire transfer. Well, mili-
tary service members are often stationed in places, both in America
and overseas, where there isn't a branch of the local bank. If you're in
Iraq and you need to send money to your family, you want certainty
that it'll get done. Military banking did that, and I knew its value to
military families better than most.

With that advantage, I blew everyone away in military sales. My
co-workers started calling me "the military specialist." Additionally,
we had just devised a new online military banking system that I was
able to pick up much faster than my boomer colleagues, most of
whom hated opening military banking accounts. They were used to
an archaic system that looked like MS-DOS. The new system was

about as hard to use as the old Myspace social networking site. Even so, my older co-workers avoided it like a disease and, in doing so, sent all those valuable customers my way. I was so good that Bank of America named me Puget Sound Seller of the Quarter in 2006.

Most customers don't know that personal banker jobs are considered sales. We sell products to you that make the bank money. We disguise it as help—and sometimes the products really are right for customers—but ultimately selling financial products is no different than selling cars. Except people *know* they are being sold a car.

One quarter, I led the region in credit card sales, which were very hard to close. I have to admit, I had some help: A new credit card had been introduced and, for reasons I still don't know, there was a glitch that allowed every single person who applied for it to be approved. Regardless of an applicant's credit situation, the application went through. I can't identify the card issuer for legal reasons, but, trust me, that company was good to me. My secret weapon was my brother, who had become a popular barber at a shop inside a mall in Tacoma. He had a crazy number of clients, and once I told them that the card issuer would approve anybody, I was able to tap into all of them.

First, I got my brother approved. That way, we knew for sure the glitch was working. My brother's credit was probably the worst since America started tracking credit. Name any detriment to your credit score, and Jason had it in abundance. Charge-offs? Check. Accounts in collections? Accounts closed out with negative balances? Check and check. He had payments due that were more than thirty days late, sixty days late, and ninety days late. He'd had cars repo'd. Whatever you need to do right to enhance your credit he'd done terribly wrong. He was a barber, so he got paid in cash, basically making it impossible for him to pay all of his monthly bill consistently. So when that man got approved for a $3,000 credit card, I knew something was wrong. Once I got Jason squared away, I got cards for my entire family, even my grandmother. *Everybody eats, B!*

After that, my brother started to spread the word to his customers. Black barbershops are the home of the hookup—the one-stop shop where you can get everything from CDs to cologne to fake college degrees. Pretty soon, Jay became the guy with the credit card hookup. And I was the plug. He kept a stack of my business cards near his barber's chair, and I spent that summer providing the whole city with credit cards, with limits ranging from $3,000 to $5,000. A few people actually used the cards to rebuild their credit. The rest just went crazy, snapping up Xboxes, new suits, whatever. I didn't care. Folks would walk into my branch, give me "the nod"—you know the nod, the one that says "Hey, you the guy with the hookup?"—and I would give them the nod that affirmed that yes, I was the man they were looking for. They would wait in the lobby to see me and only me. My manager loved it. Jay would call me with clients in the chair literally getting their hair cut. With the sound of the clippers buzzing, I would take application after application over the phone. Jay's customers would get that instant approval and be hyped!

A profitable quarter was one in which you sold ten, maybe fifteen cards. That summer, I may have sold as many as a thousand.

I'm telling you, when I was locked in, I couldn't be beaten. Problem was, I grew increasingly less locked in at Bank of America as time went on. Once I started moonlighting at Nate's on Thursdays, my passion for comedy quickly eclipsed any interest that I had in working at the bank. More and more, I spent my time trying to figure out how to get my online content in front of more people and promote my live stand-up sets. In fact, if I'm honest, there were plenty of times when they could have fired me and probably should have.

Let us recount a few of those times:

- On my first day, I fake got lost and arrived two hours late. Mind you, I'd been living in Washington State for almost ten years by the time I started at B of A, and the branch where I worked sat on a main road. Literally, anyone with eyes could find it. I didn't let that stop me, though.

I knew even before I began working there that I'd hate that job. I knew I wasn't gonna make a lot of money. I felt stuck. I was just wasting time. It was like knowing I had to turn myself in to the authorities for a crime and was trying to delay my surrender for as long as possible. I *needed* that morning before prison. So I pretended to not know the way to the office and went to another branch. I watched as they called my job to get the right directions. Once I'd assured them that I was now on the right path, I stopped by Starbucks before going in to work. Looking back, I'm sure they knew I wasn't lost.

- I used to take naps in my car on my lunch break. Even if the nap only lasted ten minutes, I had to get it in. One day, the temperature was so hot that I pulled under a covered area to go to sleep. I woke up to my manager banging on my window. Turns out, the covered area where I'd parked contained an ATM, and a long line of cars had formed behind me. My manager was pissed. In my defense, people didn't use that ATM a lot. Or so I thought.

- I used to use the color copier at the branch to make copies of flyers for my comedy shows. One time, my manager handed me one. I assumed he wanted to come to the show. I got so excited that I told him he didn't even have to pay, that I'd put him on my guest list. Turned out, he didn't want to go. He had found my original flyers in the copier, and the copier ink was now low. *Whoops.*

- Once, while on the clock at work, I took a visit to Mount Rainier. Before you judge me, google Mount Rainier. It is nature in all its glorious majesty. On a clear day, you can see Mount Rainier from miles away. I wanted to see it up close. Well, one day, I had sold an annuity to an older lady whose only stipulation for buying it was that I bring the paperwork to her house so she could sign it. She lived about forty-five minutes away from the branch—and another thirty minutes from Mount Rainier. This was my chance! So I drove to her house, got the papers signed, and then took off for another thirty minutes to get to Mount Rainier. It was as amazing as I expected. I decided to grab some hot chocolate and take in the sights. That's how much of a rush I was *not* in. When else was I gonna be this close to the mountain? Never! I regret nothing.

- One time I lied and told my manager that I was going to a community event to open accounts when I really was planning to do a midday performance. If I'm not mistaken, it was the week of Juneteenth, and there was a gospel fest on a Friday afternoon. I took paperwork and all. Now, everybody knows that when you go to these events, *nobody* opens bank accounts. It's not top of mind. It's what we'd call an "awareness play," at best. But in an effort to hide my hand, I claimed that I'd opened three accounts. I didn't think anyone would bother to verify my claim. My manager had never bothered to check before. But, much to my surprise, he actually asked to see the accounts when I got back. Understand, falsifying accounts was a fireable offense, and I had never planned to open the accounts I claimed to have signed up. But now that he wanted to check, I needed to make something happen fast. I had less than two hours to figure out how to open real accounts. Luckily, my sister, who has a different last name from mine, agreed to open one account. My homegirl Kita opened another. And my sister-in-law did, too. I had them email me their IDs, which I copied at the library. Then I went back to my branch and showed my manager. He knew I was lying. We *both* knew I was lying—but my manager had no idea how I'd come up with three real account holders. Like Denzel said in the movie *Training Day*: It's not what you know; it's what you can prove.

I eventually quit B of A, but I should've left long before I did. I stayed because in spite of my entrepreneurial ambitions, I actually liked the job for a while. The credit card hustle was a prime example . . . until it wasn't. Eventually, that scheme began to fall apart. First, the housing crisis exploded. Then I got a new manager, who sucked. My old manager had allowed us to do pretty much whatever we wanted. On Saturdays, for instance, the branch would be open from 10 A.M. to 1 P.M., and we were scheduled to work 9 to 3. But since we were killing it with the sales, the old manager let us show up at 9:55 and roll out at 1:05. The new manager? She actually made us come in at 9 and stay till 3, spending the extra hours making sales calls. Nobody wants to be bothered with a sales call on a Saturday, especially the people making the calls. Where I was locked in before, I loathed my job now. I hated feeling like I was pestering people. So I quit before they could fire me.

Fortunately, it wasn't tough for me to land another job. Within weeks, I was working pretty much the same type of personal banking gig for KeyBank. Unfortunately, they sniffed me out pretty early, realizing quickly that I wasn't there to help the bank as much as I was looking for a way to earn money while I moonlit as a comedian. Whereas Bank of America accommodated some of my mess, KeyBank had no such patience.

It wasn't even that I committed that many fireable offenses. The real problem was that I just said the dumbest things possible to a manager. One day, my area retail lead pulled me into an office and asked me about my dreams. What I should have told her was that my greatest dream was to become a branch manager and eventually aspire to work at the corporate level at KeyBank. But by the time I had started working there, I already was envisioning life as an entertainer. I thought I could get away with the bare minimum. I could not.

Instead, I told the truth—that I wanted to work in entertainment.

Then she asked why I was working at the bank. I explained that it was so that I could finance my comedy dreams. Then I added that I was planning to quit as soon as I could afford to. I literally said this to her, verbatim: "I'm just working here until I blow up." Within ninety days I was fired. I guess I should thank her for pushing me toward my dream.

Getting fired from the bank taught me a lot. Just because a job is good for most people doesn't mean it's a good job for you. If you aren't going to be engaged and/or see value in your employment, it's gonna be hard to do your job well.

The greater lesson here is probably that everybody isn't ready to hear your dreams. If you aren't ready to leave your job and fully pursue your life's passion, it probably isn't wise to tell your area retail lead manager you're just working at this job until you blow up. Not everyone is rooting for you to achieve your dreams. And some people will actively try and make life harder for you.

Another lesson is that sometimes you just don't belong at a place. For a long time, I was really upset that I'd gotten fired. I felt like my management had put my family at risk. But when I sit and look in the mirror, that job was right to fire me. I wasn't living up to my potential as an employee. They needed to get someone who was committed to that company in my position. Blaming my manager for my lack of good work was just a waste of time. I deserved to be fired and was able to move forward more easily once I came to that realization.

I even recall telling Melissa—I think this might've been the first time I ever said it her—that I wanted to be more than just a person who works a nine-to-five. Even though it was the first she'd ever heard of it, she was like, "Let's make a plan." In the back of her mind, she knew I never would be content working a regular job. She probably knew before I did that this would be coming someday.

SMALL VICTORIES

Even though I figured KeyBank would get rid of me sooner or later, I didn't have anything else to fall back on when the inevitable finally came. But, to me, getting fired seemed as much an opportunity as a setback. I was out of a paycheck—but I was also freed from the constraints of a nine-to-five. At last, I thought, the time had come for me to prove I could do comedy for real, for a living.

It helped that I had finally started to earn a little bit of money from telling jokes. I had been with Nate a couple of years by this point, and he'd started paying me for my sets. I'd also connected with a couple of small-time promoters who would put me on their bill and pay me a few dollars for my troubles. I might do a little club in Auburn for fifty bucks, another little club in Seattle for fifty bucks. Then maybe I'd do a church event. Churches, they liked to pay in fruit—and I hated getting paid in fruit. I hate bananas, and they always over-indexed on bananas. Nobody wants to pour out their heart and soul only to be paid in bananas. Your wife don't understand that you bringing home bananas after being gone all day. You need money to soften that blow, not fruit.

But there was always the consolation of knowing I was in full pursuit of my dream. *This snack is from comedy,* I'd tell myself while munching my grapes.

Even with no real job, I threw as much of myself into my comedy as I could. I networked my butt off, circulating flyers about my shows, reaching out to contacts via social media, building ties with other entertainers. I remember one time I'd gotten $50 from one promoter and another $100 from Nate. As I stood at the gas station filling up my gas tank with money I'd earned from stand-up, I could not have been any more elated. I didn't care that I was earning a pittance. I didn't care that I only had enough to get the tank half full. *Comedy,* I thought to myself as I dropped my little bit of cash on pump 3, *is putting gas in my tank!* Maybe it was a small victory, but it was a victory nevertheless. Gradually, I went from "comedy gas" to being able to pay our cellphone bills or the electric bill from comedy show money.

I never stopped looking for a "real" job, of course. My wife loved and believed in me, but she wasn't trying to starve for comedy, and neither were our children. Matter of fact, when I told Melissa about my bright idea to tell jokes full-time, her answer was a straightforward and simple "No." I knew she supported my dreams, though. As long as I could keep hitting those stages and earning my small paydays, I didn't mind doing whatever else to keep our family afloat.

YOUTH PASTOR

After my unemployment ran out, I was offered a position as a youth pastor at our church. In a lot of ways, it was an ideal fit. I was looking for a job that paid well. I also wanted work that would make my family proud (even if I found it boring): a job at another bank or a university, maybe something in city or state government. I wanted a job that my grandma could brag to other people about.

The youth pastor role was fitting, though. I had always been comfortable speaking with my peers. I was steeped in Scripture, as well as in the social culture of our church community. I cared deeply about our church members, and young people in particular. And, after going months with no work other than the occasional comedy gig, I needed money desperately. When our pastor came to me with the offer to work with kids aged twelve to eighteen, I leaped at the opportunity.

The job didn't eliminate my family's financial issues, but it sure helped ease some of the pain. The youth pastor gig paid close to

$1,500 a month, about as much as my unemployment before it expired. That didn't equal the $35,000 I'd been making at the bank, but it was enough . . . barely. Even with that extra money coming in, our family was forced to make some fundamental changes to our lifestyle. My wife gave up trips to the manicurist and hair salon. We had to quit taking vacations. And in one of the biggest changes, we pulled our boys out of daycare, which was costing us about $1,800 monthly. (Daycare actually cost $600 a month more than our mortgage!) Funny thing was, daycare had become so expensive that once we had to go without it, my little $1,500 youth pastor check ended up stretching almost as far as my old salary.

My church was kind enough to allow me to bring the boys with me. We were a small, intimate congregation, and my pastor understood my plight. Plus, my sons were good boys who knew how to be quiet when I needed them to. They'd grab up an armful of toys before we left home and play contentedly until it was time for us to leave. My pastor's flexibility was unusual even for a church leader. Not many pastors would've done what he did for me, and I am incredibly thankful that he did.

And let me tell you, I loved that job—and I was great at it. The kids loved me. I took current rap songs and I turned them into messages. I went to their basketball games. I went to their football and volleyball games. I made them laugh. I taught them life lessons. I listened to them and treated them like young adults. I really got a kick out of working with them.

Also, for the first time in my life, I started learning the Bible for myself. I'd read the Bible, of course. You weren't growing up in my mom and dad's house and *not* reading Scripture. But this time, I had begun to study on my own, with a fervor and intensity that I never had before. Pastorship is a weighty calling, and I needed to be prepared. I didn't want to give bad advice or stale answers that the kids heard from everyone else. If my kids had questions or anxieties or fears, I wanted to be the one who comforted them, who prayed with them, who guided them to a clearer understanding of our faith and a closer relationship with God.

Along the way, something else happened to me: For the first time in my life, I found myself at odds with how my own pastor had taught Christianity.

I remember one of the first lessons that I shared with my charges. It was about tattoos—which, by the late 2000s and early 2010s, had exploded as a cultural trend. The kids at our church had been inundated with messages about how sinful tattoos were, just as I had been as a kid. Getting tattoos, they'd been taught, would put you in the fast lane to hell. Yes, there were some pastors who had tattoos, but we just assumed that they were going to hell, too. Sucks for those guys. So now there's a kid under my tutelage who wants to know about tattoos? Perfect. I'll explain to you exactly why you're going to hell. Sure, I'd be willing to research the issue to better make my point to our young churchgoers, but I'd already determined that I'd fully reinforce what I'd been taught: Get ink on your body, risk fire and brimstone.

But then I start looking into tats for myself. And after long hours of study, I was forced to make a surprising admission: What I'd been taught my whole life was wrong. Nobody's going to hell for tattoos. The passage that I'd always been taught came from the book of Leviticus, chapter 19, verse 28: "Ye shall not make any cuttings in your flesh for the dead, nor print any marks upon you: I am the LORD." But I also knew that the same people who lived by that passage tended to ignore a passage three verses down, where the writer warns against eating shrimp and wearing clothes made of two different types of fabrics. Now, many of the seafood-eating Christians I know will explain their deviation from this verse by saying, "Well, that was the Old Testament and, as Christians, we aren't bound by the laws of the Old Testament." I was like, *Wait. What?* I didn't question my faith, but this was one of the first times I'd ever questioned how I'd been taught Christianity. And that set me on a whole new path of teaching. Working with those kids forced me to rethink everything I thought I knew. It grounded me deeper in my love for God, but it also granted me the space to ask questions, express doubt, and toss out ideas that I had come to realize weren't right no matter how some people want to misinterpret Scripture.

In the end, I taught them that body art was fine, at least as far as I understood it. I didn't have the power to give them permission to get tatted, but I did let them know that tats were not, according to my understanding of the Bible, a sin. And they were eager to accept my interpretation. It took me nearly fifteen years after that to get a tattoo; those kids wanted ink as soon as they turned eighteen. I wasn't their parent, but I wasn't going to tell the kids they were wrong. Fortunately, my pastor was an understanding man and, whatever our disagreements, I never faced any repercussions. So I continued along my path.

Unsurprisingly, this is also how I began to reconsider my position on one of the more incendiary issues facing Christianity: homosexuality. In addition to warning against the dangers of prawns and polyester, Leviticus, of course, also is the book of the Bible that many people turn to when they want to cast homosexuality as a sin. And that's the way I was taught: If you were gay, you're going to hell. I was told that every man who is gay was molested in the past, that they had "chosen" that "lifestyle" as rebellion against God. But as I studied, I began to wonder how, if the warnings against shellfish and mixed fabrics could be ignored, this passage continued to carry so much weight.

I'd been appointed youth pastor in 2010, only about two years after my younger son, Jo Jo, was born. (Zay Zay had come along in 2006.) I remember thinking—one of the very first thoughts I had after Jo Jo's birth, in fact—*I don't care. I don't care what this boy is or who he becomes. Nothing is going to stop me from loving this child with everything I have. Nothing or no one could ever stop me from loving him.* I thought about the stories I'd heard about Christian families disowning a gay child or kicking a lesbian daughter out of the house. If my child grew up to be gay, there was no way I'd ever kick him out of my house. If my son is gay, then he's just gay. I'm not going to love him any differently.

Having children was the first time I'd ever experienced unconditional love in the way that I thought God probably experienced it. I didn't have the answers. I just knew that from the first moment I ever held my child, whatever I had been taught about homosexuality and sin would never have any bearing on how I treated my child.

I don't know all the answers. It's hard to change the way you've thought about something when you don't have competing ideas to compare it against. I think a lot of times people are just like, *I just can't change the way I think. I've been taught this so long. I don't know any other way to think.* This is especially true when it comes to religion, because a lot of times religion becomes a de facto lens for how you see yourself. It's easier to hold on to bad ideas if you don't have any good ideas to replace them with.

Of course, some of the elders in my family don't share this line of thinking. They still think about these things exactly the way that they've taught us. Even with the way the world has changed, they are still clinging to that old way of thinking. You know how the Black community sometimes can be: We don't talk about those kinds of subjects in public. But I'm vocal. I've said a lot of these things on podcasts and in other places.

As a youth pastor, I was able to share a lot of lessons and ideas. Was I successful at it? I'd like to think so. But success isn't always defined as doing the same thing repeatedly, even when the results are good. Sometimes, you have to be willing to challenge not only how you act but how you think. I still don't have all the answers. I never will, and I'm not afraid to say that. But when I do learn the right answers, I'm also not afraid to say that I once was wrong.

(I probably should also confess that I recently went from zero tattoos to four in one year. And I fear I am not done.)

BACK ON MY FEET AGAIN: BOEING

Serving as a youth pastor was an incredible experience, one that ushered in new ways of thinking about a lot of old ideas. Just as important, it held me down at a time when our family needed money the most. But perhaps the biggest benefit to come out of my time as youth pastor is that it helped me land my next job, with one of the largest companies in the United States: the Boeing Company.

I'd applied for a job at Boeing several months before, around the same time Melissa got hired on the military side of the company's operations. She got a security clearance and everything. As for me, I think they just tossed my résumé on whatever stack they keep around in case they need to call someone in for a job later. Fortunately for me, they actually did reach back out.

While Melissa probably got her job off pure merit, I needed help. It came in the form of a Black woman at Boeing who was looking to increase diversity at the company. She'd seen my résumé, she told me when she called, and it'd intrigued her. There was no picture with the résumé. And there was no LinkedIn. But I'd listed my time as youth pastor, and this is what caught her eye. Don't ask me what made me put "youth pastor at Church of God in Christ" on my list of past jobs, because I have no idea. But I did, and it worked. She told me straight up, "I'm looking to hire more Black people here, and I saw that you were a youth pastor." She couldn't hire me on the spot, but she set me up with an interview—and that's all the opening I needed.

Yes, I am a terrible employee, because I've always had such a hard time working for anyone else. But when it comes to interviewing for a position, I know how to make you *think* I want to work for you. I have an outstanding "professional voice." Want to talk about code-switching? I was a master. Business schools should write books about how I code-switched. They should build code-switching statues in my honor. I can chum it up with the best of the good ol' boys. You interested in yachts? Okay, I can pretend I'm interested in them, too. And I am funny and likable, positive signs to job recruiters who are always asking themselves whether a prospect will be collegial and productive. I have never failed to get a job that I've interviewed for. And I wasn't gonna start at Boeing. People love Big Kev. They hire Big Kev. Sometimes they fire Big Kev, too, but they always hire him first.

This time was no different. I smoked that interview! By the time I was done pitching myself, I'd landed a job on the commercial side of Boeing in the company's office in Renton, Washington, a suburb of Tacoma.

I was what's called a scheduler, which at Boeing is essentially a glorified term for someone who does data entry. Here's how it worked: When you buy an airplane from Boeing, it's like buying a car online. Let's say you want a Toyota Camry with four doors, tinted windows, and air conditioning. You go online to the Toyota website and enter all that information. Well, buying a Boeing 737 is not that different. Southwest Airlines says, "Okay, we want ten 737-

900 ER planes." And that means a 737 dash 900, which is a bigger plane, I believe. (Look, I'm just giving an example, so don't quote me on the particulars, because I never really paid attention. I do remember that ER meant "extended range.") So basically, you're buying a 737 that could fly anywhere in the United States without having to refuel once. That's what a 737-900 ER could do. After that, you get what's called a line number, which is kind of like a VIN number for a car. Every plane has its own unique line number. I would get the order from Southwest and plug that information in to the system. Here's the plane, the carrier, the line number, the wing size or whatever. From there, I'd schedule the delivery of the plane. Later, a plane fuselage—which is pretty much like a giant empty cigar tube—would arrive by train at the factory and assembly would begin. I'd mark that down as Day One. From there, eleven calendar days later, after that plane's been worked on for twenty-four hours a day every single day, it flies out of the Boeing factory ready to go.

It was an efficient system, and it also was easy to manage. I pretty much just took information from an email and inputted it into what essentially was a very detailed Excel spreadsheet. It took about thirty minutes, which meant most weeks I was only working four hours a day. I learned to stretch tasks, turning something that might take a few hours into a daylong ordeal. This isn't to say Boeing isn't good or didn't take its time. In fact, the opposite is the truth. Because Boeing was so efficient, they made an easy, mundane job almost impossible to mess up. It took a lot of people a lot of work for a lot of years to get it that streamlined. By the time I got there, the job was easy as pie. And it was all I did.

Nonetheless, it didn't take long before I was miserable.

Commuting made me sad. Walking into the office depressed me. And being stuck all day at a desk doing a job that bored me to distraction was its own living hell. It didn't help that we were living in Tacoma, with its constant downpours and overcast skies. Worst of all, having a job meant far less time for my own projects. I couldn't make videos. I couldn't edit. All I could do was research stuff on YouTube, which I did constantly. I wasn't just watching for entertainment, either, but also to learn more about what viewers wanted and how content creators were using the platform to build audiences and personal brands. I still had dreams of making it. YouTube kept me encouraged.

I tried not to complain because I knew I had responsibilities to maintain. I was a father, husband, and provider first, a comedian second. The way I saw it, Melissa had put up long enough with my failed entrepreneurial adventures. I wasn't going to be putting myself or my family in the same position as we were when I got fired from KeyBank. There was just no way.

Plus, I had to face facts: Boeing was a great employer. Getting that job was like getting a golden ticket to work at Willy Wonka's chocolate factory. We were paid handsomely. We were treated well. We got paid vacations and all kinds of perks. For instance, we didn't even have to drive all the way to work. A van would meet us at the Tacoma Mall, which was near my house, to take us to work and allow us to save gas. (I got some of the best naps of my life on that van!) This was also good because it allowed me to pick up my sons from the babysitter at the Tacoma Mall and take them home from there.

As you'd expect, I took advantage of every feature Boeing offered as often as I could. We had a cafeteria there. I would take my lunch in the morning because I started working at 5 A.M. I was eating cheeseburgers and drinking Dr Pepper at 9 A.M. every day, which is probably when I started gaining weight. (Truthfully, I had gained weight before that, but I need to blame some of this on someone else, so it's Boeing's fault, too!) Boeing gave us two weeks of paid vacation, in addition to more time off, fully paid, during the period between Thanksgiving and Christmas. No job I'd ever had could match that. At my old jobs, if you didn't go to work, you didn't get paid.

The healthcare was great, too. I remember one time I got sick and found out that they had a doctor's office at Boeing. I think I had hives or something like that. When I went to his office, the doctor told me, "Go home for the week. I will medically give you the time off, fully paid. And you don't have to tell your boss what happened. It's a HIPAA violation if they ask, so don't tell them what's wrong with you." Kinesiologists would come to our workspaces and make sure we had everything we needed. They measured our height and arm length, and people would order the perfect mouse for our hand size. The desks and chairs suited everyone perfectly. All in all, Boeing made it very easy to be there.

And it worked for most employees. The average age when I got hired was seventy-five. Nobody gets hired there because nobody ever quits. Among our friends and family, everyone was like, *Oh, you're good. You and Melissa have made it.*

And in some ways, they were right. Melissa and I were able to buy a home. We provided the boys with good daycare and schools. I had a little more money for my side projects, whenever I got a chance to work on them. Eventually, I'd end up like a college friend of mine who worked for Boeing. He worked remotely most of the time, and nobody seemed to care. He could call in to meetings from home, work whenever it suited him, and still earn more than $100,000 a year. Early on, I'd hoped that I could eventually get an arrangement like that. I could earn my money, take care of my family, and use my bonuses and other perks to fund my plays, all from the comfort of my living room.

At this juncture in my life, my dreams were as tightly focused as they'd ever been. I knew how to be funny. I knew how to tell stories. And I was figuring out how to create content online that people would want to see. I just needed more time and more opportunities. But there was a big catch: I worried that I couldn't chase those opportunities, because I worked for Boeing and would get in trouble. Consider a few of the video titles I posted to my YouTube page during my time at Boeing: "1000 Ways to Die," "Baby Mama Rules,"

"Men: Women Don't Want Your Opinion," "Ask a Black Guy: How to Trick People into Thinking You're a Thug," "You Can't Make Love to Gospel Music," "Poor People Habits." I lived in constant fear of being called into my supervisor's office to explain those. Boeing afforded us a cushion, an opportunity to see how good life could be playing by the traditional rules, but it also was a creative straitjacket.

I never wavered, though, not after all the failures I'd endured up to that point. Having a good job that made my family proud and kept money in our pockets allowed me to not have to worry as much about when that break might come. If I kept this job, at minimum we would be okay, I told myself. I wasn't sure what the next step was going to be, but I needed to make the most of the opportunity that I had. Thanks to Boeing, I was technically a success.

Too bad I hated it.

PART THREE

Making My Chance

MY SON LIVED MY DREAM
BEFORE I DID

As I've already mentioned, I wanted to be a performer well before I ever stepped onto a stage. My daily life may have been that of an average working man tethered to suit-and-tie institutions like Bank of America. But that was only who I was on the outside, who I needed to be to feed my family. On the inside was a performer grinding away on his craft, night in and night out, eagerly waiting for that first big break that would catapult him into the bright lights of pop culture fame.

I suppose it's only fitting, then, that my five-year-old son wound up making it in Hollywood before I did.

It was the early 2010s, and I was struggling to find my break. I had just started making my YouTube content. I also was performing and editing the Playmakers video series—which showcased me, Jason, and my friend Ant Davis cracking jokes about the church. Isaiah, my older son, would be with me a lot of the time when I'd bring those videos home to work on them on my laptop. After a few months of watching me, Zay Zay started getting the urge to try his own hand at comedy. "I want to be in a video!" he'd say to me over and over. (And over and over . . .)

At first, I'd just try to appease him by promising him a chance to do something "later," never thinking that later would actually come. The boy was barely in kindergarten. You don't expect kids that age to be serious about anything other than toys and candy. But Zay Zay was persistent, and over the next several weeks he wore me down. I decided to give him his chance. So I wrote some lines based on a few bits from my own stand-up routine, told him what to say, recorded a few videos, and posted them to my YouTube channel. I didn't expect much would come of it. I mean, my audience was small back then and barely getting to know me. There was no way they'd take much interest in what was essentially a throwaway project I recorded to keep my kid happy, right?

Instead, Zay went viral. And by that, I mean blew all the way up!

At the time, most of the videos I was posting on my KevOnStage YouTube page would earn views in the three figures—the *low* three figures. Some videos drew as few as three hundred and fifty views. To this day, if you go back and look at some of my oldest stuff, posts with titles like "How to Listen to Women" (eleven thousand views) and "Man Rules" (twenty-two thousand views), you'll get a sense of just how paltry those numbers were (and, um, still are). Every now and then, the views would jump up to fifty thousand or sixty thousand for a video like "Ask a Black Guy: How to Trick People into Thinking You're a Thug," and I'd think that I was on my way. Inevitably, though, I'd put out something new and the view count would dwindle right back down to three or four thousand.

Zay Zay? He had no such problems. The first video we did, titled "Growing Up Black," earned more than two hundred thousand views. And things only got better from there. With seemingly every video we'd post, Zay grew more popular. His videos went from drawing hundreds of thousands of views to attracting millions. While I'm struggling to get eyes on my own videos about fifty-five-year-old grandmothers who try out for the Dallas Cowboys cheerleaders (two thousand views), my son is garnering sixteen million views just for sitting in the back seat of our family car talking smack alongside his little brother. In only a matter of months, I helped my precocious first child transform from unknown kid from Tacoma to "Zay Zay the Five-Year-Old Comedian," an internet sensation with his own YouTube channel and following.

And honestly, it was easy. Zay was funny, personable, and cute. He had a big personality and no problem following directions. I'd sit him down, set up the camera, and feed him lines while the camera rolled. Some of the lines were taken from my own stand-up routines, and I'd tailor them for him. For example, if I talked in past tense about something like getting whoopings from my parents as a child, I'd write his lines so he'd be saying something like, "You know how Black parents be." I used to imagine that it was how Jermaine Dupri or whoever would write raps for Lil' Bow Wow. I'd feed him for ten or fifteen minutes, then I'd just stop feeding him, jump cut the dead space, and trim away any mistakes. I knew the videos were funny, but I had no idea they'd become as big of a deal as they did.

Videos were only the start. At one point, a friend called and urged me to check out Yahoo! This was back when you'd find Microsoft News or Yahoo! on the home screen of your computer. So I click on Yahoo! And there's a headline that reads "Five-Year-Old Comedian Takes Aim at Lazy Parents" staring back at me. Then came stories that were unfairly critical, like one from *Slate* magazine bemoaning how this five-year-old Black comedian jokes about being beaten. They were jokes! I wasn't beating my boys. I was spoofing me, their mom, and our upbringings (in which Melissa and I really *did* get whoopings). I'd even thrown in lines where my son compared me to Michael Jackson's infamous father, Joe. But here was this respected publication taking seriously the wisecracks that I'd made up to come out of the mouth of a kindergartner. Things definitely got real with that one. But the views continued to mount. And as they did, doors that we barely even knew existed began to open for Isaiah.

One of the biggest actually opened not long after we posted Zay's very first video: *The Ellen DeGeneres Show* called to invite Zay on the program. I could barely believe it. It'd always been my dream to sit on the couch next to one of those famous daytime talk-show hosts, and here was my son, one video deep into his social media comedy career, being asked on to one of the most-watched shows on TV. At the same time, people are calling me up like, "Yo, Kev, is that your son?" I might not have been as popular as Zay at that point, but I couldn't have been any prouder. *He wants to do what his dad does,* I thought. Then, one day, he confirmed as much himself, telling me, "Dad, I want to be just like you." That boy touched my heartstrings with that one!

Even through our pride, Melissa and I knew we had a duty to protect our son. So when Ellen's people called and asked if Zay would be willing to come on and do a five-minute stand-up set, I had to explain to them how our process worked. "He's not coming up with this material on his own," I told them. "He's basically just repeating what I'm telling him."

Ellen's people didn't seem to mind. They kept insisting that he come on and give stand-up a try. On national TV. In front of a live studio audience hosted by one of the best female comedians of her generation. Sorry, but that was not happening. As witty as my son was, he still was only five. It would be one thing if I went onstage in that situation and bombed. I was as unafraid of failure then as I am now. But my baby? No way. I remember us passing on a couple other shows for that same reason.

Adults, even teens, are supposed to take away valuable lessons from humiliating failures. We're expected to be mature enough to understand why we may have faltered at something and use that understanding to either get better or take off on another path. Kids fail at things, too, and should be taught to persevere when they don't succeed. But those are lessons to be absorbed gradually and organically, not on syndicated television because a parent doesn't have the good sense to know when to safeguard a five-year-old.

At some point over those next few months, I did get a brief chance to see Zay in an interview setting. We went to LA, and Zay did a local broadcast . . . but he kind of froze up. It's not that he didn't talk, but he wasn't giving anywhere near the energy he put out on his regular little broadcast. I'm watching that and thinking, *Lord, I can't. I don't want my son out here getting crazy embarrassed.* We took some headshot photos of our boys and went right back to Tacoma.

Despite our cautiousness, the opportunities continued to come. Zay even got an agent. In 2012, a talent manager named Jeff Levin—who to this day is Logan Paul's manager—essentially "discovered" my son. It was the whole Hollywood "going to make you a star" type of thing. Jeff also was working as a talent manager at a place called AwesomenessTV at the time, for an executive named Brian Robbins. Brian was well-known as the creator of the Nickelodeon sketch comedy series *All That.* He had also worked on *Kenan & Kel,* the breakout series that launched *Saturday Night Live* star Kenan Thompson's career and spun off the movie *Good Burger* (and was a show that Melissa and I had grown up on). Brian had just received funding from YouTube Originals to turn Awesomeness, which was owned by DreamWorks Animation, into a channel directed at kids—a Nickelodeon for YouTube, basically. Jeff asked if we'd want to be signed to work for Brian's channel. Zay Zay and his brother, Jo Jo, would be the talent. I would write, produce, and edit sketches for them. "And you don't even have to leave Seattle to do it," Jeff promised us.

The offer was amazing. Instantly, I realized that it could be a big break not just for Zay, but for me, too. But for all my excitement, I also was wary. *This is incredible for me,* I thought, *but is it for my son? Does he want to do this?* I was down with him for as long as he wanted to perform, but I also knew how difficult and discouraging my own path had been. I'd worked for years for free (and for the occasional fruit). I'd been passed over for gigs, I'd been booed, I'd lost good-paying "regular" jobs—all of it in the name of trying to do comedy. I explained to my son just how trying it can be to entertain for a living and to have to bounce back from the inevitable failures and rejection. Zay was adamant that he wanted to keep going, so we agreed as a family to do it.

Not long after signing, we created a show for Zay on Awesomeness called *Crazy I Say,* which featured him and Jo Jo (who had become something of a co-host in his big brother's earlier videos) discussing a variety of subjects through the innocent eyes of a three- and a five-year-old. We began churning out videos with titles like "Where Do Babies Come From?," "Celebrity Tattoos," and "Ask Zay Zay and Jo Jo." The boys did things like undergo a "hip hop makeover" and talked about subjects ranging from the Olympics to fantasy football to the arrest of big-time athletes. And, just as Zay had when I first sat him down and turned the camera toward him, he wowed anyone who watched him. Zay Zay and Jo Jo's videos drew two to three hundred thousand viewers at a time on a regular basis, with his most popular clips logging as many as 1.4 million views.

For the first time, we began to see real money from our efforts. For every successful idea that I pitched that turned into a video, AwesomenessTV gave us $500. And at the rate we were going, we were pushing out at least four a month. *Oh my God,* I randomly thought to myself one day. *We are getting $2,000 a month for making videos of our kids!* Melissa and I were able to put money away for the boys' college tuition. We had them enrolled in private school. And since my wife and I were still working at Boeing, we were able to save a lot of money. All in all, it was a sweet deal. I would've been happy if that's as far as it went. In fact, that's about as far as we expected it *would* go.

Instead, our lives got even crazier.

We went on like this for a little while and then one day, out of nowhere, we get a call from Barzin Akhavan, an acting teacher at UW who was now a working actor. "Kev! Agents in Hollywood are trying to get your attention," he said. I remember looking down at the phone, bewildered. "What?" I responded. "Yeah. They want Zay Zay in the new *Little Rascals* and they kinda put out an APB to find you." I couldn't believe it so I hung up and called Jeff to see if it was true.

It was. They wanted Zay to be Buckwheat.

If the Ellen DeGeneres invitation took me by surprise, this call floored me. *The Little Rascals? All this off of one YouTube video?* I kept asking myself. When the idea really sank in, I was overjoyed for my Zay. I'd grown up loving Alfalfa, Spanky, Darla, and all of Our Gang. The reboot, planned as a direct-to-DVD film, was called *The Little Rascals Save the Day*. And my son, who'd become a certified internet sensation in less than a month, was being given a shot at playing one of the most iconic (though, admittedly, sometimes controversial) roles ever to come out of that institution.

But first we had to audition. Immediately, I sent videos to a friend of mine who was a professional actor just to get tips on how to handle the tryout. Then I got the script, set up my camera, and shot Zay saying the lines. It was so intense, but he nailed it. I sent the video to LA and waited. Not long after, Jeff Levin called again.

"Kevin, they need Isaiah's measurements," he said when I picked up.

"What?" I asked. "Who? Why?"

"The filmmakers. They need to know exactly how tall he is. Can you go to a doctor's office and have him measured?"

"Can't I just tell you?"

"No, you need a doctor to sign off on it. This is official medical paperwork."

Official? Nobody had said anything to me about Zay landing the role. But I didn't want my son losing out on such a great opportunity over paperwork, so we went quickly to an urgent care in our neighborhood and got him in to see a doctor. Later we took pictures, then sent the entire package to the movie team. From there, all we could do was wait. And wait some more. I tried not to worry too much about what would happen. If Zay got the film, it would be a great win for him. But having never forgotten how my own "big shot" at the Bay Area Black Comedy Competition had soured, I tried to stay cool. I knew what it was like to think you're about to be launched into stardom only to have everything crash down around you. Failure comes built into the entertainment business, and I didn't want to set up my boys for disappointment.

Next thing you know, Jeff was on the phone again.

"You got it, Kevin!" he said. "They're putting Zay in *The Little Rascals*! You guys are going to LA for three months to shoot a movie!"

The movie shoot lasted three months. Our family's lives would be changed forever.

MAKING A MOVE
TO MAKE A MOVIE

Needless to say, we were thrilled when we got the news about Isaiah landing the Buckwheat role in the *Little Rascals* remake. But once my initial excitement faded, one of my next thoughts was what that meant for the rest of the family. The hardship we endured after KeyBank fired me was behind us, but still fresh enough that neither my wife nor I had any interest in returning to the days of me collecting unemployment checks while hustling to land $50 stand-up gigs around the city. I couldn't bring myself to put them in that position again.

I had been prepared to work at Boeing for a minute. My whole family was proud of me, telling me stuff like, "You makin' good money! You're able to rise in the company! Y'all set for life!" And I was still happily doing stand-up comedy while making my social media content. Perhaps at that point I didn't have the following that my son had amassed (okay, fine . . . I absolutely did *not* have the following that my son had amassed), but people were putting some respect on KevOnStage's name. Best of all, I didn't have to endanger my job to do any of this. Now, though, I was being forced to figure out how I was going to travel to Hollywood for three months for my son's movie without walking away from all of that.

But here's how I also viewed it: We had a good life, yes. I always believed, however, that one day we could have an even better one—and I was willing to take a chance to do it, even if it meant falling on my face.

In my mind, we really only had one choice: Zay and I were going to LA.

I took a leave from Boeing. A few weeks later, Isaiah and I moved to LA, while Melissa stayed behind with Josiah. Because we were coming from out of town, the studio filming the movie agreed to give Zay a $5,000-a-month stipend to live on. We were shooting the movie on the Warner Bros. lot, and the nearby studio housing cost $5,000 a month to rent. We wouldn't have any of the stipend left over for anything else. So, even before we left, I'd found a studio apartment for us in Anaheim, about twenty-nine miles away from the Warner Bros. lot in Burbank. Remember, I'm from Washington. I don't know much about LA. In Washington, if something is twenty-nine miles away, it takes a twenty-nine-minute drive to get there. Twenty-nine minutes wasn't that bad of a commute. When I told Jeff Levin about my plan, he quickly explained the folly of my thinking.

"Kev, no," he warned. "This isn't Washington. It'll take you an hour and a half, if not longer, to get to set. If you're lucky, it might take you twenty-nine minutes to get from an apartment in Burbank to the Warner Bros. lot—in Burbank."

Instead of Anaheim, Isaiah and I wound up in a one-not-even-bedroom apartment a "quick" thirty minutes away from the film lot. It was a studio apartment that just had a kitchen and bathroom barely separate from what was supposed to pass as sleeping quarters. The only door in the entire place that closed was the door to the bathroom. "Fully furnished" (which meant a couch and kitchen appliances), the place was barely affordable.

Zay's stipend would be just enough to cover the cost of our place and dinner. We would eat breakfast and lunch on set. By the grace of God, they had an amazing budget for craft services. Did I take stuff home to stock our cabinets? Who wouldn't have? They did this thing called "pass-arounds": Near the end of the workday, they would have sandwiches or some fried chicken. I ate that every time. Luckily, Zay Zay was small, so he didn't even eat much. I don't know that we could have made it otherwise.

Even so, my son and I both appreciated the moment. He had already done great in the YouTube space cranking out weekly videos for Awesomeness. Now a real movie studio was paying him to star in a Little Rascals movie. Even if nothing more came out of this experience, it was wonderful to be on the journey with my son. It made for a fun time and a dope adventure, even if it meant holing up in what amounted to a broom closet.

My son and I dubbed the new crib the ManPad.

MISSING MELISSA

Moving to Los Angeles marked the first time that Melissa and I were separated for a long period. I wasn't used to being without her, and it was tough. We had some rough moments. There was the time her plane got struck by lightning on the way to visit us, and she was forced to turn around and take another flight. I was terrified when I found out, but ultimately she and Jo Jo made it to LA unharmed.

As gut-wrenching as that was, the emotions paled in comparison to how I felt when, weeks after I had moved out, my mother-in-law tried to move some other man into my house—with my wife! Her mother hates this story, but it's funny . . . and it's true.

First, you have to understand that she didn't mean anything foul by it. Melissa's mom is the sort of person who's always trying to help everybody in the neighborhood. So one time, while I'm in LA with my son, my wife called and was like, "Hey, we have an old family friend who is experiencing a hard time, and my mom wants him to move in with us. He and his wife are really going through it, so my mom kind of offered our house to him while he figures it out."

My reply came as soon as she finished. "Absolutely not."

I went on: "I don't care what's happening to that man. No disrespect, but if he moves in, then me and you are going to be having a tough time. I'm not letting . . . *No!*"

"Kevin, I grew up with him."

"Yeah, that's how it always starts. 'He was my brother.' I am entirely too insecure to allow that," I confessed.

Thank God that didn't end up happening. I'm pretty sure her mom wasn't happy with me. I. Did. Not. Care. That nigga was *not* moving in my house while I was a thousand miles away shooting a movie.

THE FATHER-AND-SON
FILM DEBUT

We had a ball making the movie. Zay made a great Buckwheat, and he loved the whole experience. Just as impressive, he was as professional as you could expect a grade-schooler to be. He showed up on time, prepared. He handled his lines well. He got along with the other children. And when we weren't shooting the movie, we would get to do cool father-son stuff all the time. We'd go out for pizza and check out movies, go sightseeing in LA.

He did say that the whole thing was harder than he'd thought it would be. The days were long, and he struggled a little bit after one of his teeth fell out. He'd already shot some scenes with his tooth intact. For the sake of continuity, they couldn't very well have scenes where Buckwheat has a tooth missing and others where he doesn't, so he had to wear a bridge in his mouth that gave him fake teeth. When he first got it, he cried because it was so uncomfortable. He never really got used to the way it felt.

Watching and talking with Zay, I came to realize that, as much fun as he was having, acting wasn't something he felt like he had to do. I never thought, *Oh man, I know he's going to do this for a living.* It was more of a ride-this-for-as-long-as-we-can type of feeling.

For my part, I was awed by the sheer scale of Hollywood productions. For the first couple weeks, we'd go on location, and the production team would place these little yellow signs that would say the name of the movie and then point in the direction of the set. So, if you were driving to this location for the first time, these signs would be there to make sure you didn't get lost. Even on days when we weren't shooting or when we were driving to set, I would see those signs everywhere. So it was in my mind, I'm like, *This is just a whole industry. Movies are being shot all over the place here. It's not just ours.* The sheer size of it all blew my mind.

But the best part for me? I wound up in the movie myself! They were running short on funds toward the end of shooting, and they needed a montage of the kids trying to raise money to save their town. They couldn't afford any extras, so one of the producers comes over to where the kid actors' parents are gathered and makes an announcement: "If any parents want to be in the film, let me know!"

I was like, *Oh my God! You guys* have *to be talking to me!*

I ended up playing a doctor in the movie. I didn't have any lines, but I had to squeeze a syringe, and one of the other actors, Connor Berry, the little Black kid who played Stymie, would pass out. That was my first big movie break: squeezing a syringe.

I went back to the ManPad and immediately called my wife. "Lis, they're going to let me in the movie!" I told her. "I don't think my name's on the call sheet or anything, but I'm in the movie!"

Even better, my scene survived the final edit. I remember one of the producers saying, "A movie is not made until you're watching it in theaters" because he'd been a part of movies that were shot but they couldn't finish the edit or they couldn't get distributed or whatever. Up until the moment I saw myself in the movie, I figured my scene might be cut out. By the grace of God, I made it.

To be honest, my screen time in this film is about 2.5 seconds. All I did was lift a syringe and press it till some liquid spurted out. If you sneezed one time or blinked too long, you could miss my entire performance. But was it an Oscar-worthy display of acting prowess? Absolutely! I should have won an Oscar, Emmy, Tony, Grammy, Dove, and Country Music Award for my performance in *The Little Rascals Save The Day* straight-to-DVD movie.

Would you believe that I run into acting teachers who saw my role and said that they play my scene for their students as an example of how you make every moment count?

No? Good, because that part's a lie—but they *should*.

HOW PUMPKIN PIE NEARLY COST
ME MY BLACK CARD

My film cameo aside, it seems like my and my son's careers couldn't have been traveling in more opposite directions in the early 2010s. In 2013, for instance, while Isaiah was becoming an internet darling, wooing TV executives, and attracting film roles, I got myself mixed up in an online controversy that even to this day has some people questioning my very Blackness.

All because I once publicly admitted in a video that I like pumpkin pie.

I didn't think much of the notion when I shared the clip. As I mentioned earlier, pumpkin pie was one of the mainstays of my childhood, along with *Star Search* and church services. I grew up on it. Love it to this day.

How was I to know back then that Black folks aren't allowed to like pumpkin pie? With us, it's all about sweet potato pie, especially when it comes to the holidays. To most Black folks, pumpkin pie is like potato salad with raisins in it or an unseasoned turkey, which is to say that not only is it out of step with Black tradition, it's something of an affront.

Simply put, pumpkin pie is for white folks.

So when I innocently shared how I'd grown up eating pumpkin pie, I was not at all ready for the level of offense that niggas took. It was as if I'd said bridge was a better card game than Spades or that Rocky Marciano could outbox Muhammad Ali or that Larry Bird was superior to Magic Johnson. Never mind that my roots are in the South and I've always been solidly in step with the Black community on all important matters. I grew up in an old-fashioned, sanctified Black church. I'm grounded firmly in the Black gospel music (and comedy) tradition. I'm raising my Black sons with my Black wife.

I said I like pumpkin pie and instantly got treated like I called cops to the cookout.

Honestly, I don't know why Black people have such an adverse reaction to my love for pumpkin pie. There's a story to my preference for it, but Black people don't want to hear it. They don't care. *Your Black card is on the line.* But see, my mom was not much of a baker. So from Halloween till Christmas, basically, when I would come home from school, my mom would have pumpkin pies on the kitchen table. She would just go to the grocery store and buy 'em, and they would just be there for us to take a little slice. I thought nothing of it.

When I talked about it on social media, all I ever said was, "I like pumpkin pie." I didn't disparage sweet potato pie at all. It wasn't an either/or for me. All I said was, "I like pumpkin pie."

Folks immediately came for my Black card. *"Sweet potato pie is better!"* And to me it wasn't like sweet potato pie vs. pumpkin. But just the fact that I eat pumpkin pie, in the Black community, this is sacrilegious.

And here's the funny thing that nobody wants to admit: Maybe not all, but a large percentage of pumpkin pie haters have never even *had* pumpkin pie. They just be like, *"I can't trust you!"* And the trust goes beyond food. They're like, *"I don't even know if you voted for Obama . . ."*

They don't trust your Blackness because of a dessert choice.

Over the years, I managed to turn the controversy to my advantage. I started making it a running joke. Nowadays, since I know I can get a reaction out of Black people, literally every fall season, I start reminding them that I like pumpkin pie. And new people find out every season because my following is still growing. So it's treason every fall. Every holiday season, it's like I'm storming the Capitol of Black desserts again.

People act like I'm talking about pumpkin pie versus German chocolate cake. The pies are not that different. They're both orange vegetables. Pumpkin pie is usually just less sweet. Black people, we like our desserts sugary sweet, and pumpkin pie is usually not served as sweet as sweet potato. But that's why it's called *sweet* potato pie. That's why "sweet" is in the title. Yeah, it's sweeter—because we make everything sweeter. You ever looked at the back of Kool-Aid packets and see how many cups of sugar they recommend—and then see how many cups Black people put in? It's crazy. Of course it's sweeter. Everything we do is more. Everything we do is in excess. So now I just do it to antagonize people every holiday season.

People don't take nothing else this personally. People are not nearly as upset that I don't like German chocolate cake. Nobody cares. I don't like bananas. So I don't eat banana pudding. Nobody cares. And you know what I do my videos for these days? I do them for all the Black people who are afraid of being bullied by sweet-potato-pie-loving Blacks. I do it for all the children out there who are afraid to live their truth. I will be their champion. I'll be their martyr. That's why I will never back down.

But yeah, when I first came out, everything about me was called into question. Black people wouldn't trust my judgment on anything. If I'd say, "Oh, I don't like this song," the response would be, "Of course you don't. I mean, you like pumpkin pie."

FLIPPING THE WORLD

Zay's movie was released on DVD not long after filming wrapped. We always knew it was going to be a direct-to-DVD deal so we never figured much would come of the actual film. And not much did. It didn't earn much critical notice, and it certainly wasn't a huge commercial success. For most people involved, it was a moderate payday for just another run-of-the-mill Hollywood reboot. For my son, it marked a memorable experience that he'd cherish but quickly move on from. He was super proud of it. We were very proud of him, but we knew the movie in and of itself wouldn't change his life much.

None of us had any idea, though, that it would completely alter mine.

It happened quickly, too, long before we left to go back to Washington. By the time we were wrapping up the film, I'd already decided that I was ready—no, that our family *had*—to move to Los Angeles. Immediately. It wasn't just one of those hazy, distant dreams, like the scenario I'd concocted about being discovered at the Bay Area Black Comedy Competition. This was an urge. A calling. I simply had to be a part of what was going on here. The sheer size of the movie-making space at Warner Bros. had left a deep impression on me. But the moment that truly inspired me to move was far more subtle, so simple a story that most people probably wouldn't think it'd affect me as much as it did. In fact, it stuck with me forever.

We were on the *Little Rascals* set one day, and I was watching the crew closely. Since I'd never been on a movie set before and knew nothing about video production, I always was like a kid in a candy store whenever we showed up on the lot. I paid close attention to everything all the time. On this particular day, I watched as the crew members set up the lighting, noting how skillfully they made use of basically one camera aimed in one direction, how they shot each line from the script. It was amazing to see how the process worked.

Then they started getting ready to use this trick where they would turn the cameras around and shoot the reverse of what they'd just filmed before. It was a process they called "flipping the world." Depending on the time of day, how many cameras are being used, and so forth, flipping the world can take anywhere from fifteen minutes to half an hour. So I'm standing around with the crew while they're getting ready to flip the world, and I catch sight of this random sound guy, who's just waiting around like everyone else. He rests his boom pole on his work carts, pulls out his cellphone, and just starts playing a game on his phone right there. Then he calls his wife. He's like, "Yeah, I'm on break. We're flipping the world, then we're going to lunch soon." It was something simple like that. After he hangs up, he places his boom pole in its case and goes back to playing the game on his phone.

And that moment—the image of that man putting that boom pole in the case and getting out his phone to play again—is forever engraved in my mind. What I saw in that moment was the normalcy of life in this sprawling, complex organism called entertainment, and that's the life I wanted to live. I needed to be in a place where my job was something as cool as shooting sound for a movie. I had spent my adult life working jobs where the break room was a small office surrounded by other offices. I wanted a job where when anybody takes a break, your break room is a set on the Warner Bros. lot. I wanted to be in a place where those little directional signs line the street, where movie sets are coming to life all around you. It was no longer enough for me to while away my life in Tacoma, dabbling on the periphery of entertainment. I wanted all the way in. *I've got to make it in this city,* I told myself.

Talk about flipping the world.

Looking back, I'm not sure that I'd ever taken the idea of "making it" nearly as seriously as I should have. I'm not saying I hadn't tried, with my plays, my videos, my eagerness to do stand-up at just about any place where you could fit a mic and an audience. I'd sacrificed some good jobs. Even now, at the Boeing job that I'd regarded as a blessing, I couldn't come to grips with the notion that punching a clock for a faceless corporation was my destiny in life, no matter how good the health benefits. I appreciated my job—but I also hated it because it represented a barrier between me and the world I longed for. I'd felt stuck between obligation—in my head, I knew I couldn't put my family in another financial bind to chase this crazy dream—and ambition. Now I was going to make a move. I had dreamed before. I had suffered. But now I planned.

I called Melissa that same day and told her that we had to move to Los Angeles. And then, over a series of emails that I fired off while Zay and I were still in Burbank, I laid out exactly how we'd do it.

THE FREDERICKS FAMILY
MANIFEST DESTINY PLAN

Okay, first things first. Yes, I know the name of the plan sucks. I shouldn't have called it that. The idea of Manifest Destiny— that white Christians had a God-given right to exploit Native Americans and steal their land in the name of westward expansion across the United States—caused a lot of harm to a lot of people in this country's history. It's a terrible idea, and I want people to know that I'm aware.

At the time, I didn't know any of that. It just sounded grand, sweeping. I was hoping to sell my family on the idea that we could quit our cushy white-collar jobs at Boeing, uproot our family from Tacoma to Los Angeles, and dive headlong into the entertainment business. I needed Melissa to share my vision, so I wrote out and presented her with my blueprint, politically incorrect title and all.

Now, before we jump into this plan, let me remind you that I am a church kid. I may joke a lot, but I actually was ordained as a minister around 2008. Having been a pastor—even if only a youth pastor—I knew that a move this serious was no joking matter. This was my family's future. So I went full preacher mode. I went before the throne of grace. There was not one joke here. Melissa and I joked before and after I presented this plan, but these paragraphs reflect serious biblical business.

Fredericks Family Manifest Destiny Plan

I believe that God has given us an opportunity to fully utilize the gifts he has given us and to have a life we have only dreamed of. I believe our new life is just around the corner and with planning and faith we will reap the full benefits of God's plan for us.

The Scripture I'm basing this decision off of is Genesis 24:27:

Blessed be the Lord, the God of my master Abraham,
Who has not left my master bereft and destitute of His loving-kindness and steadfastness. As for me, going on the way [of obedience and faith], the Lord led me to the house of my master's kinsmen.

The servant activated active dependence. He was sent to find a wife for Isaac and he embarked on the journey, but depended on God to guide him to the right woman.

That's exactly what we are doing; we are embarking on the journey toward our destiny. What God has planned for us is bigger than Washington, bigger than a greater life, it's even bigger than you and me. We have a place in his plan for the nation, for the world. We are walking in thy path.

The following is my beginning plan which will be the launching point for the move:

Our House

I called the realtor. He's going to send us over the documents that will explain the process in detail. He says our best play with the bank is to tell them that we had to move because of our jobs and couldn't keep up the payments on both residences and we could not sell our house. He says it is in our best interest to not pay the mortgage to make it more obvious and just save that money for the move. He can have a lock on the door within a week. I told him once we see the paperwork we will take the next step. Whatever we save can be applied toward the move.

Moving Costs

I spoke with two moving companies and without seeing how much stuff we have they both gave me an estimate of between $2500 and $3200. I scheduled a walk-through for the week before Thanksgiving to get a written quote. One of the moving companies quoted me an additional $1200 for the car. But I got a quote from a car moving company that quotes $490. So total move, roughly:

$4300 all within moving company

$3600 moving company and car company

They will disassemble and reassemble or move to storage. (I think there were also smaller costs for a few minor expenses I've long since forgotten.)

Our Jobs

I believe it is in our best interest to stay with Boeing at least through the Employee Incentive Plan. I believe even if we began applying for jobs in December we will have enough time to negotiate a new start date after we receive EIP.

I would think it easiest to take a Boeing job in Long Beach for the time being. Not having to worry about new stuff. If we look outside of Boeing, I recommend living in the Valley. That's where we are living now. It's 45 mins to downtown LA in traffic, not to mention jobs we may find in the city we live in. Burbank, North Hollywood is considered the Valley.

New House

Based on my estimates, we need to be ready to at least pay $1,500 for a decent apartment in the Valley. This price was able to rent us a nice house in the Long Beach area when I first looked. Once the Discover card is paid off, I believe we can cover that.

School

Isaiah's school will be disrupted for a little bit. But we both went through similar things as military kids. I went to a lot of elementary schools; sometimes I moved during the school year. Honestly, I don't even remember that much about first grade. At this pace, it's more likely that Isaiah will be homeschooled rather than attend traditional schools.

Church

We love our church and have been committed. This move isn't about sticking it to them or anything like that. This is about following our dreams and doing what's best for our family. We love them, we will always love them, but we have to move on.

I think we can take some time and visit a couple different LA churches. What's most important to me is the message being taught and the children's church program. We can visit one church at a time, Noel Jones's church, Bishop Ulmer's church, Bishop Blake's, and Bishop White's churches. I think after a couple visits each we can talk and make a decision.

Update

Since the beginning of this email another moving company called and quoted as low as $1300. I told him what we are taking. Since we aren't taking refrigerators and other large appliances, it will be cheaper.

Job Search

We should start doing some soft searching getting an idea of what's open, what parts of the city, salaries. We should start applying shortly after I return. Boeing first, then others.

Living

We should do soft searches and get an idea of what we can get for what we want to spend. What I mean by soft searches is checking prices. Not necessarily filling out paperwork. When you are down here the next two times we can look in person or I can take video. The process has already started. We are moving on. Along the way God will be with us. He is always with us.

And that was it. That was my brilliant idea for getting my family out of Tacoma.

In hindsight, so much of that plan is hilarious to me. I was being hasty, hadn't thought everything through the way I should've. But I was determined. And fortunately, my wife was with me. Melissa always knew that a day like this would come, the day when I finally decided I couldn't take working for other people anymore. Being in LA had switched off any interest that I might've ever had in going back to an office in Tacoma. I was too far gone now, and my wife knew it. She was willing to support me, to make the big move, but she also didn't hesitate to point out that parts of my plan were, well, dumb.

Prime example was our house in Tacoma: Since we weren't likely to keep our jobs after we left Tacoma, I wanted to walk away from our house—and our mortgage. We had just bought our home two years earlier, in 2008, and the house was upside down by about $30,000, the consequence of the recession and of us not having any money to put down on the home when we bought it. This meant that, to sell the house, I would have had to return $30,000 to the bank. I didn't have an extra $300, let alone $30K, so selling the house wasn't an option.

I knew walking away from the debt would do serious damage to our credit. But, hey, I'd worked in banking before. I figured I'd come up with a plan to help us dig out and restore our credit once we found an apartment in LA and got on our feet. I'd make so much money that we could pay for things in cash until our credit was right. I was ready for this struggle, I insisted. I was ready to risk my house, my Experian score, all of it.

After she read over that part of the plan, Melissa offered another idea: "Kevin, instead of letting the house go into foreclosure, why don't we rent it out? That way, we can still pay the mortgage here and keep our credit intact until we're ready to sell."

Duh!

The way I reacted, you'd have thought my wife just discovered fire. *Oh my God! Of course! We can rent the house for what we pay in mortgage, maybe even a little more to make a profit!* Silly guy.

Lis's amendment was Exhibit A of how my ambition could blind me to the obvious. Because of her, we were able to find a renter—and then another renter when that tenant couldn't rent anymore. We kept our house in Tacoma, and it's now worth more than double what we paid for it. If not for her, not only would we not have had that equity, but we would've also had a foreclosure on our credit history and no house. That's just one of the million examples of where listening to my wife has been tremendously beneficial.

Even when we disagreed on a part of the plan, she never wavered on the overall mission. Through it all, she had only one clear-cut demand: Wherever we moved to had to have laundry on the premises. There would be no apartment building laundry rooms, no coin-operated wash-n-go's, no trips to friends' houses to do quick loads. She didn't want to be lugging around two small boys and a bunch of bags anytime they threw up on something or peed on the bed. It was like, *I believe in you—and us—and I know it's going to work . . . but I will not live in a place that doesn't have a washer/dryer in the unit.*

I understood. So, with that demand in mind, we set about leaving everything we'd already made real so that we could chase a dream.

THE KEVIN FEDERLINE MIX-UP

During much of our time working for AwesomenessTV, before and after our move, the platform served as equal parts classroom and workplace for me. I learned a lot about drafting sketches, shooting skits, and attracting larger audiences via YouTube and social media sites. I made some great contacts. I also continued to try my hand at writing scripts, hoping that one day I'd be able to successfully pitch any of the countless ideas I had for movies and plays. That never happened for me over there, but it sometimes led to some humorous moments.

For instance, there was the time I got up enough nerve to pitch a movie directly to CEO Brian Robbins, the mastermind behind all those hit TV shows and films. Since he'd hired my kids to work for him at AwesomenessTV, I decided that he might be open to turning one of my screenplays into his next big hit. In my head, it didn't matter that I didn't know the first thing about screenwriting or that the movie idea almost certainly sucked. Brian and I had become cool enough that I felt comfortable approaching him with ideas. I decided that I was gonna take my shot.

I remember printing out the script one day and confidently walking it over to his assistant. I watched her take it from my hands and walk through the glass door that led to his office. I watched her set it on his desk. And then, for the next few months, I proceeded to "bump into" Brian all around the office and wait for him to acknowledge my screenplay. I didn't want to bring it up, and, even if I did, I didn't really know how to broach the subject. Instead, I kept waiting for him to say something.

Months go by, and he never says anything about it. *Okay, this must just suck,* I finally concluded. *He doesn't want to make it, which I'm not happy about, but hey, this is Hollywood. It is what it is.*

A couple more months go by. Then, one day, we're casually in conversation in the office—I think we just happened to be walking past each other—and I said to him, "Yeah, man, whatever happened to the movie? Obviously, you didn't like it. What happened?"

A confused look spread across his face.

"Movie? What movie?" he asks.

"The movie I turned in to you. I handed it to your assistant and haven't heard anything since. I was just curious."

Surprise quickly replaced confusion on his face.

"Ohh, man! That was you?" he said. "Man, I thought that script said Kevin *Federline*. I threw it in the trash. Didn't even open it."

I was incredulous. "Brian, are you serious?"

"Yeah, man. I'm sorry. I looked at that thing so fast, saw the name 'Kevin' and just tossed it. I was wondering, though, why in the heck Kevin Federline was trying to pitch a script for a kids' movie."

My excitement for the movie had passed by that time anyway, so I didn't bother pressing him about it. I don't know that there was any real lesson about failure in that experience, but what I took away was that sometimes you just have bad luck.

I guess it could be worse. I could actually *be* Kevin Federline.

GETTING SETTLED

Upon moving to Los Angeles, we found a small apartment in Reseda, a neighborhood in the San Fernando Valley, that cost about $2,300 a month to rent—$1,000 more than the mortgage we carried on our house back in Tacoma. It featured something called "tandem parking," which I'd never heard of before. You got two parking spots, but they were back-to-back instead of next to each other. You'd have to block one of your cars in when you used both spots. And, of course, there was a washer/dryer in the apartment.

The neighborhood itself was a little, how do you say, *Grand Theft Auto*-esque. There was a car wash right next to our apartment where I am certain I witnessed at least a few low-level felonies after sundown. Now, I ain't no snitch—but my policy was challenged not long after we moved in, when our apartment was robbed. They stole my kids' piggy banks, which were replicas of actual pigs, so these criminals had to know they belonged to children. Still, they stole them. The funny part is, the thieves didn't take any laptops or cameras. They stole literal pocket change. But hey, welcome to America. We made it work.

We chose Reseda partly because it was about thirty miles away from a Boeing office, and our plan called for us both to relocate to a nearby Boeing plant and commute to work, same as we had in Tacoma. We knew the commute would be brutal, but we still underestimated Southern California sprawl. Once we realized that a thirty-mile drive could take up to three hours, we had to rethink employment. By the grace of God, Melissa got a job at an aerospace manufacturer that was fifteen minutes away.

I tried to get back on at Boeing—we both did—but there were no jobs in or near Los Angeles. At Boeing, you don't just transfer. You work on specific aeronautical programs, so if you leave one location, you get transferred someplace they make the same planes. I'd hoped to go to the El Segundo facility, but it wasn't the same program, so I couldn't just transfer in. I would have to apply for the job like everyone else—and, as a hiring manager explained to me when I decided to leave Tacoma, time spent working elsewhere in Boeing did not count in your favor. Worse, they weren't even hiring at the El Segundo plant. If I still wanted to be a scheduler, my best shot was at a facility in Columbia, South Carolina. After all we'd done to relocate to Los Angeles? Wasn't happening.

So once again, we were looking at the prospect of struggling until we could right the ship financially. Fortunately, Lis had gotten her job, and I was still under contract with AwesomenessTV, earning $2,000 a month shooting and editing the boys' videos. Sure, money would be tight for a while as we navigated LA. Everything had to be budgeted to the penny. We couldn't even afford a flat tire—but as long as we were working, we'd figure it out.

Imagine my surprise, then, when AwesomenessTV dumped us.

AWESOME NO MORE

Losing jobs has never been a source of panic for me. As I said earlier, I can accept that I'm not many people's idea of the model employee. Most of the times I've left a job, it was because I hated what I was doing and refused to do anything more than the bare minimum. Sometimes, like with KeyBank, I got caught doing things that I shouldn't have been doing. I don't think I'd ever lost a job that I loved, primarily because I'd never loved any job—until the day AwesomenessTV decided they didn't need me and my boys anymore.

I loved the work I got the chance to do for Awesomeness. I spent valuable time with my sons. I put out content that we created and controlled. I got my first credit as a TV writer by writing and directing my sons' sketches. And I was gaining valuable experience about how to leverage social media platforms to build the KevOnStage brand.

To top it off, we were winning. Our viewership numbers for segments like *Crazy I Say* were strong, usually in the high six figures. The Little Rascals movie that Zay Zay starred in had helped make his and Jo Jo's clips more popular than ever on YouTube. They'd even appeared in AwesomenessTV sketches that were aired on Nickelodeon. Everything seemed to be going smoothly. So after a couple of years, when our contract with Awesomeness was set to expire, I assumed I'd have at least a little bit of leverage when time came to negotiate a new deal.

I'm going to go in there and negotiate a stronger contract, I told myself as the negotiations neared. *They mean X, Y, and Z to the network, and I know they're deserving of at least double.* The way I envisioned it, the boys were going to get a raise. I'd get a raise, too, as writer, director, and producer. Everyone would be treated fairly and according to their true worth.

My wife wasn't so sure that things would work out that way.

"Are you sure they value you the way that you *think* they value you?" she asked gently.

It was a short and simple notion, but it flew right over my head. I had decided that views and comments were the tangible things they would be looking for, so I never doubted myself. I fully intended to ask for what I felt was ours. And that's what I did. I went in and asked for double what we were being paid. I didn't think bumping us up to $4,000 a month was too much to ask.

Instead, they released us from our contract. Didn't counter. Didn't just re-up at what we were already being paid. AwesomenessTV just let us go.

To say I was stunned would be an understatement. "Wait a second," I implored. "I was planning my life out based on this money. We're doing really well, so there's no reason not to keep going. If you're not going to give us double, at least just give us the same."

Nope. After two years, it was over. Their rationale was that, while we created entertaining content, we weren't the influencers that AwesomenessTV needed. They wanted more talent that came with a social media following already built in so that they could use that following to promote their programming. But here's the rub: After signing Zay to a contract to do content for them, AwesomenessTV had prohibited us from hosting that content on my son's own YouTube page. All our good stuff went to their platform exclusively. We had stunted the growth of his page—and his followership—because that's what they'd told us to do. I didn't care at the time because nobody else was offering to pay us two grand a month. Now, though, our acquiescence was being used to undermine our value to them.

As disappointing as it was, it also proved to be an important lesson. When it comes to business, playing the part of the enthusiastic, rah-rah worker isn't enough. And I also learned that you have to be careful about overvaluing yourself. The best thing you can do for a negotiation is understand how the *other person* values you. Some people might say that I overplayed my hand, but I honestly felt like I was asking for what was fair. Given that they didn't even renew the deal we'd had for two years, I'm pretty sure they'd decided to release us before we even started talking about the contract. No amount of haggling was going to change their minds.

Fortunately, even though I was disturbed by the contract talks, my boys didn't really care. They both were tired of it all anyway. They'd had a good time, but being on set was a tiring experience. Also, the bigger their show got, the longer the shoots became—and the less time we were at home. Later, they admitted that they just wanted to be kids, not working professionals. The first videos we made, we did that stuff for fun, but when it becomes a job, it feels different. So just as quickly as their careers began, they were over. We might've done a few one-off things, but that pretty much was the end of their run. These days, they're just regular teenage boys who were once internet sensations. I like to say they're retired now.

That was the end for them. For me, the grind had only just begun.

MOTEL NAPA

With or without AwesomenessTV, our struggle in LA was epic. We were staying afloat, but barely. Nothing came easy for us, not even having a good time.

Take, for example, this one vacation to Napa Valley that I planned for me and Melissa, not long after we'd moved to California. It was one of the rare times we found ourselves with a little bit of extra money—one of us had earned a bonus or something. Since we'd had a rough go of things after leaving Tacoma, I decided that my wife deserved a trip someplace nice. All my life, I'd heard about the beauty and classiness of wine country, and I had seen all the movies that were shot there. It seemed like the perfect getaway, so I told Melissa, "I'm taking you to Napa Valley for two days!"

A key part of our plan was that we would trim costs by skimping on lodging. The idea was to hang out in Napa, enjoy all the sumptuous perks of the wineries and restaurants and shops, and then rest our heads at a cheap hotel. But all the nearby hotels we were seeing were $350, $400 a night. I think we only had about $1,000 total. At that rate, we'd be out of cash before we could enjoy food, wine, or anything else. The only rooms under $100 were at a budget hotel in Napa—no, it wasn't even in Napa; it was in some place *near* Napa—so I tell my wife, "Hey, we'll just stay there. At least the wine will be nice."

When I tell you this was one of the most disgusting places I've ever stayed, I am not exaggerating. Mind you, we traveled on the cheap a lot when I was younger. We never stayed in great hotels, maybe a Courtyard Marriott that we got for block rates of $80 a person for church council meetings—that kind of thing. But I had never encountered any place as repulsive as the facility Melissa and I found ourselves walking into this day. The motel room doors faced the outside. You could hear the highway traffic roaring all night. When we first opened the door to enter our room, we stepped inside only to realize that there was no carpet on the floor. Somehow, though, the place still smelled like eight thousand Newports had been smoked in there, and more were being puffed across the rest of the premises. A couple of the rooms were available by the hour, a clear sign that illicit activities were happening at this place. Unquestionably, butt was on the menu here. They would leave the light on for you, all right. The red light for sex.

Thankfully, the rest of our trip was nice. We saved enough money to enjoy the wineries and some good food. But that hotel was a grimy reminder of just how far we had to go to have the life we wanted. After that, we agreed, "We can't do this again." Melissa and I promised ourselves that if we wanted to take a trip but a place like this was the only hotel that we could afford, we were just not going.

PALM SPRINGS COFFEE

One bad trip wasn't going to deter bougie Kev from enjoying his discount luxury vacations. Being broke might have put some restrictions on how much I could indulge, but I was going to find a way to get out and see the world around me.

Like the time we traveled to Palm Springs for Melissa's birthday. God, that place was so expensive! I can't remember our exact budget, but when I tell you it was tight, I mean to say we had absolutely no margin for error. We probably wouldn't have even made the trip if I hadn't called her father and asked for his help. "Pops, we ain't been able to do nothing," I explained. "And I really want to take her someplace nice." So he gave me $500. The rooms at the resort were $300 a night. He covered one night and some food, and I paid $300 to cover another night.

Melissa and I knew going in that we had to be extra careful with our disposable income. Thanks to me, we didn't even make it through breakfast before our budget got blown up.

Our first morning at the resort, we went down to this restaurant at the hotel. We thought they'd be serving continental breakfast, so when the waiter comes by and asks if we want coffee, I order a cup and my wife requests a cup of tea. We figured coffee and tea were complimentary. They weren't. The resort was charging for every-thing. Coffee and tea were eight dollars a cup. Of course, I didn't find this out until we'd already started sipping. I panicked when the waiter mentioned the price. *Sixteen dollars for coffee and tea?* I didn't have it.

I went looking for a manager to talk to. Sheepishly, I explained that I didn't know there was a charge for the coffee and tea and that I didn't expect the drinks to cost this much. I was completely embar-rassed. They looked at me like I was a poor orphan. It felt like they could tell I wasn't trying to run game on them. They knew I was just flat broke. They basically saved my life by taking that coffee off the bill. I knew we didn't have the money to be where we were, but I didn't expect to get exposed in such a humiliating fashion the first morning of our stay.

Still wasn't as bad as that nasty motel not-in-Napa, though.

ALL DEF DIGITAL

As real as our struggle in LA was, I remained determined. Not once after our move did I give serious consideration to returning to Tacoma—not when AwesomenessTV refused to renew our contract, not even when we were flat broke. I remained confident that if I continued to work hard, my break would come. I wasn't afraid of failing. Heck, I was used to that. But what I would not do was surrender.

I held fast to my conviction that proximity was the name of the game. The closer I could get to the heart of the entertainment industry, the better my chances of breaking through as an entertainer. Turns out, I was right. The biggest break that I got in my early career, bigger even than the movie role or the AwesomenessTV deal, came simply from working in the same building where a big idea was being born.

When I was creating content for my sons for AwesomenessTV, I learned of another hot digital startup that was brewing only a few doors down from our offices. The name of the operation was All Def Digital, a video content platform that was being created in partnership with AwesomenessTV as the first major hip hop channel on YouTube. Under the deal, All Def also would provide content to HBO and Facebook. Just as important, All Def was headed up by one of the most powerful men in entertainment, Def Jam Recordings co-founder Russell Simmons. The man who'd turned acts like Run-DMC and LL Cool J into international icons and helped transform hip hop into a billion-dollar global phenomenon was now about to dive headfirst into digital content.

All Def had investors, and YouTube itself reportedly had sunk an initial half-million-dollar stake into the company. They had a ready audience waiting. And they had a plan, which was to fold the property into the same portfolio of YouTube Originals where AwesomenessTV was placed. The channel promised to be funny, edgy, youthful, and Black. In some ways, it seemed, it'd be the AwesomenessTV of hip hop. From where I stood, it seemed they had everything they needed—except for me. I determined that I'd rectify that oversight.

I wasn't sure how, at first. I didn't know anyone at the startup. The closest I'd ever come to Russell Simmons was watching him on my TV each week as he closed the show on *Def Comedy Jam*. Furthermore, word about All Def was spreading, and it seemed like every young Black content creator around wanted to be part of it. This was early in the digital content game, and there weren't many other channels that catered to the hip hop audience. The competition to land a job there would be ferocious. But I knew that if I could get on with them, writing sketches, doing comedy, whatever, I would be that much closer to succeeding in entertainment. Plus, I found out later that they'd be paying $1,000 per minute for each sketch, which was unheard of. I really needed that money.

To my surprise, simply meeting Russell Simmons wasn't hard at all. One day while I'm in the hallway of the Santa Monica building where AwesomenessTV's offices were, I spot him walking by with some of his staff. I don't know what I would've said to him on my own, but just as he neared, a colleague of mine popped up and waved him over.

"Oh, Russell," my co-worker said, "you should meet Kevin. He's really funny, and he's doing some great stuff for AwesomenessTV!"

Russell was polite, if brief. He shook my hand, asked how I was doing, and told me he'd heard good things about me. Then he continued to move down the hallway. I'm sure he doesn't even recall meeting me that day. But for me, that brief introduction was so emboldening, it might as well have been a gilded invitation. After years of toiling at small comedy sets and putting out low-cost YouTube videos on my own dime, after years of struggling to have my plays seen and my jokes heard, I saw in that hallway meeting my chance to step fully into digital entertainment—and do it with perhaps the most famous name in hip hop. In years past, I wasn't always ready for every opportunity that came my way, but this was my time.

I took small steps at first. In 2014, after weeks of calling Russell's assistants to set up an initial appointment, I finally got a chance to pitch my ideas to All Def executives. I talked them through two sketches I'd come up with, one that ran four minutes and the other a two-minute idea. And they bought both, for $6,500. Part of me couldn't believe it. If I was surprised at AwesomenessTV paying me $500 for a sketch, imagine my astonishment at getting $6,500 for two that I knew would only cost me a fraction of that to make. *Oh my God, this is crazy.* The first two sketches I'd ever offered up to Russell Simmons's team were a hit in the boardroom.

Unfortunately, the sketches never aired. For all the excitement people like me had about this new hip hop platform coming online, All Def seemed to be plagued with problems from its beginnings. I can't remember exactly why they shelved the sketches, but I do recall there being a sense that the channel's content was offensive, stereotypical even. It wasn't that my content in particular was problematic, but the channel got backlash early that made some of the executives gun-shy about airing edgy sketches. As a result, they had started nixing projects all over the place. But they paid us in full, so, as bummed as I was about not seeing my sketch on air, I was still pumped about the potential of All Def.

I got another shot not long after that, when I went in to pitch a movie idea to Russell and his team. The movie, whose working title was *Bad Little Brothers* or something like that, was a comedy that featured Zay Zay and Jo Jo as a pair of unruly kids who constantly get into trouble while being babysat. (This was before my sons decided to retire.) The idea was based on a sketch I'd done for AwesomenessTV with another YouTube collaborator nicknamed Spoken Reasons, who'd begun collaborating with All Def Digital almost from its inception in 2013. At the time, Spoken Reasons was one of the funniest and most popular comedians on YouTube; I'd considered it a huge coup to get him to do the sketch.

Titled "Where's My Milk?," the sketch features Spoken Reasons trying futilely to get the boys to behave over breakfast after they realize they're out of milk for their cereal. The skit garnered nearly nine million views and was so popular that we followed it up with a second skit we dubbed "Babysitter's Nightmare." (I played a small role as the stepdad.) The skits did so well, in fact, that Spoken Reasons and I quickly adapted them into a feature film script and convinced his manager, Loud Records founder Steve Rifkind, the man who'd brought the world the Wu-Tang Clan, to set up a meeting with Russell in hopes that All Def would produce the film.

Russell agreed to have us come to his house to pitch the idea. I played it cool with Rifkind and Spoken Reasons when we got the news, but I was so giddy that, as soon as I got the chance, I called my wife and gushed like a little kid going to the mall to meet Santa Claus. "Oh my God, Lis, I have the address to Russell Simmons's house! He started hip hop! This is going to be dope even if nothing ever comes of it."

My fortunes were finally changing, my career finally starting to get liftoff. As I saw it, working with one of the biggest Black YouTube personalities of the early 2010s represented a significant step forward. In less than three years, I'd gone from headlining a Thursday night comedy set at a restaurant in Tacoma to writing sketches for Russell Simmons's multimillion-dollar digital entertainment company. LA was still a struggle, but the scales were starting to tip in my favor.

Spoken Reasons and I went over to Russell's place to pitch him, but the conversation wound up being so much more. Yes, we also talked to him about how to find the audience for the movie and how to market it to them in the modern digital space. We explained that Isaiah was fresh off the Little Rascals movie and still had momentum as a child star that we could capitalize on. Soon enough, we found ourselves pitching not just a film but a marketing strategy for the entire All Def Digital brand. I urged him to recruit other top influencers, like Timothy DeLaGhetto. I shared my thoughts on how he should set up payments to content creators. I dropped name after name of potential talent, writers, editors, administrators, and executives. I wasn't trying to impress him. I'm not sure that I even was consciously aware of it in that moment, but so much of the time I'd spent thinking of how to promote my plays, raise my kids' YouTube profile, and produce my own content had left me with keen insights into digital marketing, especially to Black audiences. Now all the knowledge that I'd quietly accumulated over the past few years was spilling out in this extemporaneous info dump in the middle of Russell Simmons's living room.

And it was working. I don't know if I can say Russell was mesmerized, but his focus was intense and unwavering. Long after we figured the meeting would be over, we were still sitting there talking to him and answering question after question he had about how to upgrade All Def. When the meeting broke up, Russell followed me out the door, asking who else I knew, how I had learned the information I'd shared with him, and what other recommendations I might have. As usual, I called Melissa right after the meeting: "The pitch went great! I don't know what's going to happen, but I don't know if it could've gone any better."

A few days later, my phone started ringing, showing an incoming call from a 917 area code. I was busy, so I ignored it. To this day, I never answer a phone call if the phone number is not already in my phone or if I don't know to expect a call from a number with an unusual area code. Most times, it's just spam anyway. But then I saw that I'd received a voicemail. It was from Russell. (I didn't even know he knew how to get my number.) And he was excited.

"Kevin, I love what you said," went his message. "Give me a call back as soon as you get this."

So of course, I immediately called back. Russell picked up right away. I barely got my hello out before he started talking.

"Man, you really impressed me with what you know about the internet during that movie pitch," he said. "I'm trying to build All Def up, and you really seem to know what you're talking about. I don't know about this movie, but I could use you at All Def. Why don't you come run content for me?"

I was as stunned as I was excited. As was so often the case in my life, I'd set out to do something—in this case pitch a movie—and failed at that thing, but somehow also discovered an opportunity I never expected. As Russell's offer lingered momentarily in the air, I felt as if everything I'd worked for had dovetailed into this. This was why I'd been so restless at so many jobs, why I had quit Boeing and the bank, why I was telling jokes in restaurants and coffee shops, why I had jumped at the *Little Rascals* movie offer.

I'd left Tacoma for LA on a whim less than six months ago. Now, with Russell's proposition, I felt I was about to arrive.

AWKWARD BEGINNINGS

Even though Russell Simmons himself had invited me to join his new digital venture, there were still a few hoops remaining that I had to jump through. The biggest and most critical was a job interview the company had scheduled for me with its new CEO—a tech guy from another channel whom Russell had brought on—and the rest of the C-suite.

I had heard of the guy even before meeting him, and I knew that he was sharp, informed, and straightforward. Where many of the early digital platform leaders were former television executives who'd brought with them habits and POVs still rooted in TV industry culture, this guy was among the first executives to have a solid understanding of digital as its own medium. Most of his peers only knew how to make things with TV budgets and veteran TV creatives. But in digital, especially when you're a small-time creator, you have to know how to make things with little to no budget. For instance, on a television show, you have five to ten minutes to set up a storyline. In a feature film, you get twenty-five to thirty minutes. On the internet, you have three seconds to set up the premise.

Russell's new hire was just the guy to come aboard and take the company to the next level. I remember telling Melissa that he was brilliant. If Russell followed his lead, he was going to make All Def a major success.

When I showed up to interview, it became immediately apparent that the All Def executives weren't nearly as impressed by me.

"Why should we hire you?" one of them asked point blank as I ran the meet-and-greet gauntlet. "You have your own YouTube page, but you haven't made it. You're basically a failed YouTuber. How would a failed YouTuber be able to help me build a company?"

Wow. Okay then.

I could've taken offense or gotten flustered. But as insulting as the question might've seemed, I understood. We were talking about a multimillion-dollar operation that had already gotten some stinging criticism. Russell was trying to rebound and help carve out a larger role for hip hop–themed content in the digital space. YouTube and AwesomenessTV had significant stakes in the company. They needed to get hires right—most especially the spot I was going for. As the content director, I'd be given a staff and oversight of almost everything that All Def churned out. I'd also have a hand in producing, writing, and editing. With the new CEO determined to bring the operation in line with digital standards, I would have to manage the budget carefully. The days of paying $6,000 for a five- or six-minute sketch were ending. I needed to prove to the All Def brass that this "failed YouTuber" could handle the responsibilities that came with leading their team.

I gave him a basketball analogy:

"Phil Jackson is one of the greatest coaches of all time, right? And he also was in the NBA, although no one would ever argue he was a successful NBA player. Sometimes the best, most successful coaches are the ones who didn't get a lot of chances to play, so they spent more time watching. They understand the game differently than a player who's just amazing at the game. That's why Jackson will be a better coach than Michael Jordan—because Michael Jordan could play so well that he didn't have to worry about how certain things are taught or learned, not the way lesser players like Phil did."

It wasn't a prepared response. It was an idea that I honestly believed, and he knew it. Failure hadn't just humbled me. It had taught me to understand where I'd gone wrong and inspired me to show others how to not make the same mistakes. Doing videos with low views taught me how to grab people's attention. Shooting long videos and seeing how a creator with jump cuts does better compelled me to adjust my own shots. Had I succeeded from the jump, I wouldn't have learned as much. They say you never learn from a victory—but you learn a lot from a loss.

Anyway, the All Def exec loved my answer. I'm pretty sure it won me the job.

All Def offered me the job immediately, and of course I leaped at the chance. But even after all that, the job wasn't quite all mine. It wasn't until the first day I actually started working there that I learned that I had been hired to replace someone who hadn't yet been fired. I started on a Monday. My predecessor's last day was scheduled for the Friday of that same week. That meant we'd have to spend my first and his last week at All Def working side by side. Worse, nobody had told him yet that he was being let go. As you can imagine, the situation was super awkward.

The whole time, I was consumed by this misplaced sense of . . . I guess *guilt* is the best word. It wasn't my fault this person was being fired. Russell's team had made that decision even before I came on board. But I still knew that my opportunity had come at the expense of this other person's job. Why hadn't anyone warned me? Why hadn't they just brought me into the office the Monday *after* they canned him? It felt devious and underhanded. Not exactly the way I envisioned the start to my big break.

I never found out why exactly they'd fired the person who came before me. All I ever heard was that they were never sure he was "the right person for the job." Of course, what was unspoken in that comment but also understood was that I, too, had to prove that I was the right person.

That first day set the tone. From that moment on, I never felt safe at All Def. It wasn't a reassuring environment. I always felt like I was a couple of bad sketches or a couple months of bad numbers away from getting fired. You know that old saying, "How you get 'em is how you lose them"? I'm thinking, *One day somebody's going to be replacing me, and I'm not even going to know my replacement is working here.*

THE HATERS

All Def was cutthroat. Everybody wanted his or her shine. Everybody was jockeying to get noticed, to write the funniest jokes, to create the skits that would go viral and earn the bosses' attention. Good-paying digital jobs in LA, especially in the hip hop space, were almost nonexistent at that point, so our staffers were desperate to hold their posts.

Meanwhile, it was my job to oversee that office. As the head of a twenty-person team, I was responsible for supervising the writers and ensuring that sketches got made on time and within budget. I also had the final word on whether sketches were approved and made it online. Given my sudden authority and the fact that my predecessor had been run out, it wasn't much of a surprise when I quickly became a target.

Barely two weeks into the job, people started to complain about me. It wasn't everybody. In fact, it really boiled down to two particular people on our creative team, both of whom had proven to be incredibly talented and impressive. I don't think they had any real beef with me—they barely knew me. More likely, they wanted to be the people in charge, and I was the guy standing in their way. Whatever the case, they made sure they made their displeasure about me known to Russell Simmons whenever they could. They didn't trust my judgment, they told him. They didn't think I was funny. They didn't believe I had the talent to get the most out of our team. Oh, and I was "too much of a Christian."

It was this last complaint that baffled and annoyed me most. To me, being a Christian wasn't a drawback as an entertainer, but a plus. In Seattle and Tacoma, I'd fashioned my church experiences into the cornerstone of my stand-up sets. My KevOnStage commentary, my Playmakers videos, my sketches with my family, all of these had been drawn from my everyday life as a steadfast believer. Yes, I'd failed spectacularly in some of my efforts. But every time, I'd gotten up stronger, smarter, and funnier than before. As a result, I'd amassed a growing YouTube following, put my son in a movie, and built an online brand being the very same Christian comic who was now, according to my co-workers, too corny for All Def.

As off-base as I thought the criticism was, there was nothing about the complaints that shocked me. My faith had been an issue from the time I began at All Def. Russell himself used to remark all the time that I was a Christian executive running a hip hop site, as if it were the oddest pairing he'd ever seen. He used to say things like, "Oh, well, Kevin, he's a Christian, so . . ." or, "We've got this Christian guy in charge . . ."

Russell also loved stoking conflict. He didn't believe in an office where employees backstabbed or insulted each other in private. If there was a problem, Russell wanted everything laid out on the table. You don't like this person? Russell would pull y'all into a room to talk about it. You had a beef with how someone ran a department or edited sketches? Russell would force you to work it out.

Unsurprisingly, then, it was only a matter of days before he was summoning me into his office, along with the two co-workers who'd complained about me, to hash out the dispute. I walked in, sat down, and, with my two would-be saboteurs hovering nearby, Russell got straight to the point. "Yo, Kev, they think you're a corny Christian nigga and that you aren't the right person to be running talent at All Def," he said. He wasn't mincing a single word. I sat silently.

I figured my co-workers would take the cue Russell had given them to start listing all the things they hated about my leadership. But instead of standing on what they'd told Russell, my co-workers began backtracking right away.

"No, no, nooo, we weren't saying *that*," one of them stammered.

Russell cut him off. "Naw, don't try to change it now. You said he was a Christian nigga, and he can't get the job done."

When he was done, I smiled and offered the calmest reply I could muster. I can't remember my exact words, but basically, I reminded everyone that they're entitled to their opinions and that I had come to All Def to do the best job I could. I praised their work and did my best to counter their arguments about my judgment and my sense of humor while trying to be as diplomatic as possible. When we were done, I thanked them and Russell for sharing their honest opinions and got up and left. I couldn't show it, but I was pissed off and shaken.

Dang, I thought as I walked back to my office. *These niggas really trying to get me fired!*

I hadn't even been at All Def a month.

It was a lesson learned, though. All my life I'd been told that not everyone will like you. Sometimes, it doesn't matter what you do or how you talk to them. Some people just don't want to see you thrive. Sometimes they're driven not by malice or resentment but by a genuine feeling that they're more deserving than you. People have all kinds of stuff running through their heads, and you'll drive yourself crazy devoting any real energy to trying to figure them out.

Instead, I realized that my job was to keep doing my best irrespective of circumstances or co-workers. They hated me and were vocal about it, but I still had a job to do. Had our relationship been online, I could've just blocked them. But this was the real world. I had to keep showing up and figure out how to work with them—or around them—so we all could win. I didn't have the power to fire them. Instead, I adjusted . . . and I waited them out.

THE WORK

In retrospect, I'm sure part of the reason some people worried about my faith was because, starting off, we were doing work that, frankly, did conflict with my beliefs. We did some good content back then, but we also put out a lot of videos—about Black people twerking, say, or about the relative size of Black men's penises—that were problematic for any number of reasons.

The tension I felt wasn't just about my religious beliefs, but also about how I wanted to see Black people portrayed in popular culture. And I wasn't alone in my concerns. Even before I'd gotten to All Def, critics had slammed some of the earlier stuff as stereotypical and trite. Sadly, we'd continued to churn out content like this even after I'd arrived; only now I was as responsible for it as anyone else.

For All Def back then, the name of the game was scale and numbers. Our success depended on how many eyes we could get on our content and how fast we could grow that audience. As a result, we sometimes put out videos that we knew played to the lowest common denominator in the name of capturing eyeballs. Consider, for instance, a series we used to do called *Is It True?* It was a clip in which we'd get people together to discuss and test social theories that a lot of people just accept on their face. There were some good ones, where we explored the truthfulness in colorful and lighthearted topics like "Canadians are nicer than Americans," "College grads are smarter," and "Most Americans can't pass a citizenship test." Unfortunately, that segment also was used to fuel some stupid and harmful ideas, like "Latinos make better tacos," "Black guys prefer big booties," and "All Black guys are good at basketball." We did distasteful things like blindfolding guys and having them feel on girls' butts to determine how much they liked them. It didn't take a panel of us to sit around and weigh in on these silly notions to realize that some of our topics had been drawn from tired racial mythology.

However, I confess that I wasn't voicing many objections. Two weeks into the job, the last thing I needed was to be seen as a malcontent or as a disruptive force. I had sacrificed too much to risk getting fired on principle. I was the dude who'd gotten fired from KeyBank and quit Boeing so he could chase opportunities like the All Def job. My kids had to eat. So, even though I had the power to shoot down content, I allowed a lot of sketches I didn't like to make it online because I wanted acceptance . . . and my paycheck.

Many co-workers felt similarly. I heard from plenty of creatives who didn't like some of the content that we were producing but had gone along with it because they wanted to keep their job or improve their odds of moving up in the company. We were doing stuff like "Is it true Latinas are the best kissers?" and "Is it true fat girls cook better?" Oh my God, just thinking back on it is embarrassing.

And to make matters worse, we were sometimes dishonest about it. Once we did a segment that looked at the "truth" behind Black people and camping. The idea we were selling was that Black folks don't camp. But all the people we were casting were Black people who'd actually gone camping before! We were asking them to fake it so that we could peddle an idea that was a lie to begin with.

Over time, though, we made changes. As we built our audience, the crasser videos became fewer and fewer, until finally we were able to stop doing that kind of stereotypical content altogether and produce more of what those of us on staff actually wanted to see.

One big shift that helped me immensely was our decision to cut back on sketches where we used outside actors and focus more on unscripted comedy content that featured in-house talent. Initially, it was more of a business decision than a creative one, as a single sketch could run All Def anywhere between $5,000 and $10,000. Using our in-house talent with our unscripted material, we could produce four or five videos at the same price it cost to create one sketch. Not only that, but we soon realized that our unscripted material garnered just as many views. What began as a cost-saving experiment became our calling card.

Best of all, we produced our new stuff without any fears of humiliating ourselves or denigrating our communities. Not only was our work funny and cost-effective, it also was original, authentic, and worth the time it took to create and consume it. One of the prime examples is a show we created called *Great Taste,* which I had a hand in shaping. *Great Taste* features various members of our team sitting around debating some of our favorite low-budget food, from the best fried chicken to Top Ramen noodles. At first, it was meant to feature only two people talking, but Patrick Cloud, one of my colleagues, worried that nobody would want to watch two people going back and forth, so I came up with the idea of adding a "peanut gallery" to distinguish the show from other debate-style programming. It was an instant hit.

Perhaps the best and most enduring example of our creativity during my time at All Def was a program we put together (and that still airs) called *Roast Me.* The setup was simple: We put a crew of the sharpest-tongued comedians on our team in a mock classroom and turned them loose to start insulting one another. It was a straightforward and uncomplicated idea, one that hearkened back to Black folks' time-honored tradition of sitting on a porch, in class, or at a table in the school cafeteria, playing the dozens. Even now it continues as one of the most popular programs ever on the All Def channel. One thing that makes it so hilarious is that nobody is safe. You get to see some of the wittiest comics anywhere good-naturedly tearing into each other with rapid-fire, no-holds-barred wisecracks.

. . . like the time the team decided to roast me by zeroing in on the size of my head (which, for the record, ain't *that* big). Oh, they had their way with a brother, for sure.

"Kev was jogging on the freeway and got into a head-on accident!"

"Kev got sad and his pastor said, 'Keep ya head up!'"

"If Kev was a producer, he'd be 'Heady' Riley!"

"Kev ain't need a GPS; he already knows where he's headed!"

Hilarious, organic, spontaneous, *Roast Me* was everything we wanted in our unscripted programming but could make happen only after we'd made our sea change. Once we got rolling, the atmosphere at the office improved. I think people started to recognize and even appreciate what I could bring to the team. Despite my turbulent start, over time I won the trust of the troops. That trust crystallized into friendships that've lasted to this day.

We had a group of eight people who were willing to do it all: write, produce, act, and edit. Eight people all on the same wavelength. It was me, Pat Cloud, Megan Thomas Williams, Tahir Moore, Trevor Wallace, Dreezy, DoBoy, and the late great Teddy Ray. We all were of the same mindset, had a growing audience, and felt an even greater determination to make fresh content that we could be proud of. None of us were huge on the internet yet—especially in comparison to the other people we worked with—but we were on our way. I learned that working with like-minded people who are willing to agree to the same vision is considerably more valuable than having a couple of high-priced people who just want to take your money.

We knew coming in that All Def had huge potential. Now it was time to fulfill it.

AUDITIONING FOR ISSA RAE

At one point while I was at All Def, I thought I was about to become a TV celebrity. I'd received an email saying that Issa Rae, the brilliant actress and producer who created the series *Insecure* for HBO, wanted to see me *personally* on the set of her hit show. *This is it!* I thought. I was about to hit it bigger in Hollywood than I'd ever imagined. Kev was gonna be a star, a recurring character on one of HBO's biggest prestige comedies. I was bragging to people at work, telling them how my whole life was about to change. *So long, suckers!*

Unfortunately, I hadn't bothered scrolling all the way through the email. It wasn't until later that I realized I'd missed the part where it specified that I was being asked to come in for an audition. So I auditioned. And I didn't get it. My friends at work never forgot. What's worse, another friend of mine did land the role! (He was right for it. I wasn't.)

To this day, I've never booked a job through an audition.

KEV ON WEED

In the summer of 2014, I feared I might be on the verge of drug addiction.

Mind you, up until then, the closest I'd ever come to being high was the time I snuck a sip of champagne at a wedding at age sixteen and, years later, when my wife and I each took a shot of Patrón Añejo at age twenty-nine. We expected the liquor to send us on a full-on LSD trip—but instead we just wound up turning off the lights in our studio apartment in Burbank, staring at the ceiling for twenty-three minutes, then falling asleep. Not exactly the stuff of an Alcoholics Anonymous testimony, I know.

By 2014, though, we were ready to try the hard stuff. Melissa and I agreed together that we'd take a chance on an experiment that, if my most far-fetched fears were correct, could land us either in the graveyard from an ugly overdose or in a rehab center struggling to get that monkey off our backs.

We decided to try *weed*.

I chuckle now at the notion of getting strung out after hitting one joint—but back then? As curious as I was, I was just as apprehensive, not to mention feeling a little bit guilty. Don't forget how I was raised: Although marijuana was legal in a number of states by the time we first decided to try it, I had grown up in an extremely strict Pentecostal church that believed drugs were of the devil. According to my church, there was very little difference between weed, heroin, cocaine, LSD, and ecstasy.

Part of me was terrified that I'd wind up like Jamie Foxx as Ray Charles in rehab. I pictured myself looking haggard, face sunk in, eyes heavy-lidded and sullen, wandering around aimlessly in search of one more hit of a weed joint.

Anyway, you let me get sidetracked, but I needed you to understand the foundation.

By the time we'd decided to experiment, Melissa and I had made our abrupt move to Los Angeles, marking the first time that we'd both lived away from our extended families. LA was where we became full-fledged adults. At some point that summer, we got this bright idea to send our kids to visit our parents—half of the summer with my mom and dad, a couple weeks with her mom and dad. We'd have six weeks of our own to do whatever we wanted. Even though we were still pulling ourselves together financially, we promised to travel and do things that we could never do while the kids were around.

One day, I had the bright idea that we should smoke some weed.

In our minds, it would be like a second chance at a college experience—because during our first one, Melissa and I were too terrified to have any actual crazy college experiences. Back during our real college years, our idea of a wild night was to hit International House of Pancakes late at night. Come 10:37 P.M., we would look at each other and say, "Do you want to go to IHOP?" Then we would go and order a short stack (because: broke) and when the pancakes would arrive, we would say, "Our parents have no idea that we are at IHOP right now!" We would snicker about that, eat pancakes, and go back to our separate dorm rooms. To us, that was being rebellious. Sex? ABSOLUTELY NOT! We weren't heathens! But eating that short stack on a Tuesday night at 10:37? That was living, baby.

Now that we were adults, we had time to be rebellious for real. We were gonna smoke! Problem was, I didn't know how to get the weed. I had heard of having a "weed man," but how do you actually go about procuring one? I didn't want anyone at my job knowing that I was planning to smoke weed. I considered the dispensaries. There was a spot called MedMen, a weed store in downtown LA that apparently was like the Apple Store. And I love Apple products. But what if someone I knew spotted me in a MedMen? Then people would know that KevOnStage was gonna do a weed smoke. I couldn't risk being caught buying weed.

If this was gonna be my first weed smoke, I wanted it to be special. But how? You can't exactly tweet, "Hey, I would like to purchase one weed for smoking purposes." Even if that worked, everyone would know. And what if it was laced with something? Would we die? I like being alive. So, how does a church kid with a huge platform get weed to smoke?

We brought our dilemma to Melissa's brother and sister-in-law. They had the solution. It just so happened that they had recently sworn off smoking and had some "pre-rolls" left over. Of course, they then had to educate us on what a pre-roll was: a joint that already had been rolled with a good amount of weed molecules to smoke. This meant we wouldn't have to fret with preparing our own joint or blunt or whatever they're called. Perfect.

They came over to hang out one night and left the pre-rolls at our house. I took one loud sniff and thought, *This is certainly weed!* It was musty. Kinda smelled like grass combined with the scent of the crevice between your ball sack and your thigh after a particularly sweaty day. *This is it!*

I carefully placed the pre-rolls in my top drawer for safekeeping. We couldn't just smoke them on the first day we got them. That felt like addict behavior. So we went the whole summer without smoking them. Day after day, week after week, we knew they were there, but we couldn't gather the nerve to smoke them. Next thing we know, the summer has flown by and our kids are getting ready to come home in less than seven days. *We got to smoke them! It's now or never! If the kids come back, we will destroy them and never have this opportunity again!*

So one random night, I say to Lis, "Let's smoke some weed." What the heck, here's our chance. This is like going to IHOP in college. Our parents don't know we are doing this. There's one problem, though: We don't know how to smoke. Like, how do you get it in your body? We don't want to be coughing all over the place. We took a couple puffs, but we were just holding the smoke in our mouths. So we did what all sensible Americans do when they don't know how to do something. We YouTubed it: "How to smoke weed."

I still remember the video instructions. "Light the joint. Take a deep breath. Let the smoke fill your lungs. Hold it . . . That's what's gonna get you high. Then when you can't hold it, exhale."

And that's what we did. Well, that's what I did. Lis gave up. Weed smoke wasn't for her. But me, I was determined. I gave it another try. I drew in a deep breath. Smoke filled my lungs, and I began coughing like never before. My chest felt like it was on fire. Surely, I would end up like Jamie Foxx as Ray soon enough, but I could deal with that later. Tonight, I was going to smoke me a weed and get high.

I took another puff. Success. I was now a weed smoker. *This is great,* I thought, *but I'm not high.* I puff and puff and puff. I'm still not high. It's just that suddenly things are . . . funny. Like, have you ever thought about raccoons? They are funny. I said "raccoons," and it sounded like Richard Pryor in his prime. Funniest thing ever uttered. *Raccoons.* I'm not high as I write this, but I still stand by it. Raccoons scurry when they are caught red-handed. *Scurry*—another funny word. "Raccoons scurry," I repeated. *Man, that's funny! I am having the time of my life even if I'm not high.*

The next morning, I was still convinced I hadn't gotten high, until my loving wife showed me the video she had recorded while I was not-high-but-just-thought-that-raccoons-were-funny-especially-when-they-scurried. My eyes weren't just bloodshot. They were swimming in a pool of red. Raccoons weren't just funny when they scurried. The thought of breathing made me laugh hysterically. The video had several long minutes of me trying to convince my wife that I was *not high* by bursting into fits of laughter at things that no sober person would ever find funny. Doors. Doorknob stoppers. *Pfbbbtbbttttt,* the sound door stoppers make. They were just *Showtime at the Apollo* to me. HILARIOUS.

So yeah, I smoked a weed one time. But that was no match for the time I ate an edible because of my wife. Now, *that* was high for real!

Once again, allow me to set the stage. By that point, my first weed smoke was six or seven years in the past, and I was planning to never again do anything related to marijuana. I was okay with that. Never smoked again, never had the urge, hadn't crossed my mind in the least. It was a funny story that happened once, but I'm done with that part of my life. I've kicked my addiction—until we go on vacation with some friends.

Vacations are usually when Lissa and I try to do something wild. "International waters," we always joke. Usually, that means drinking a little too much, doing reverse cowgirl in the hotel living room, and then falling asleep. I mean, we *are* church kids at heart. There's only so far we can ever really go.

But this time is different, and it's wholly and completely Melissa's fault. We're in Mexico with friends, so something crazy is definitely possible. I'm hoping to have sex outside. Feeling the cool breeze brush across my butt would be fun. That is *not* what happened.

Instead, this is the part of the story that shows just how fast things can change. We were all in the hotel room. I think it may have been six or eight of us. I can't quite remember. (That's what drug use does to you!) I do recall that the hotel had laid out a welcome spread of food for us. Charcuterie boards, fruit, chips and guacamole, a couple finger sandwiches, fufu things like that. So I grab some pineapple and put it on a plate. Just then, Kirk Franklin calls me.

Kirk and I have been friends for years now. When I was starting out in social media, I used to occasionally make funny videos poking fun at him, and he loved them so much that he ended up following me on Instagram. That alone was a huge thrill for me. To church kids, Kirk was like our Michael Jackson. The greatest musician ever. At first, he would just comment on some of my posts and keep it pushing. But then, during the pandemic, I started doing a segment I dubbed *Theological Thursdays,* where I would interview assorted people about issues related to Christianity. One Thursday, I interviewed a theologian who had some views that seemed dramatically different from what the Bible usually teaches. Someone who had an opposing view urged me to get a different opinion and actually reached out to Kirk about getting in contact with me. Kirk got my number and got on a call with me and a few others, almost like it was a Christian intervention of sorts.

Ever since then, Kirk has randomly called and texted to check on me and to let me know he's proud of me. This time wasn't much different.

Ring ring.

I look down and notice it's Kirk calling. We're friends, but it's still crazy to me that the biggest gospel superstar in the world is calling my number. I tell Lissa who's on the line, then I answer and step outside.

"Wassup, Kirk," I greet him.

"What's up, King!" he shouts. "I just wanted to tell you that I love you and I'm proud of you. You are doing amazing things for the kingdom. Keep going. If you ever need anything from me, you know I got you. Just let me know. I am here to serve you."

"Okay, Kirk! Thanks!" Then we hang up.

Kirk has done this at least once every three months for the last couple of years. The calls never last more than two minutes because I never ask for anything. It's just dope of Kirk. And this time, his call was no different. I stepped outside. He said his stuff. We said good-bye, and I came back into the room to eat more crackers, cheese, prosciutto, and those little pickles.

Only this time, when I get back to the room, everybody is laughing and talking about how Melissa is so crazy. I laugh that nervous kind of laugh, the kind you give when you don't know yet why you are laughing but you want to be included in the joke.

I'm like, "So what did she do?"

Again, my friends erupt in laughter.

"She took an edible!" someone says.

I'm sorry, what? Edible?! I've been gone for two minutes. When did we get edibles? Who smuggled edibles out of the United States? I mean they are legal in LA, but now they've been smuggled. Also . . . What?! Melissa never even finished the joint when we smoked years ago. She's never been high. Why did she take an edible?

"Lissa, you took an edible?" I ask.

"Yup. International waters," she says.

But we hadn't discussed this. I didn't know "international waters" now meant drugs. Maybe butt stuff, but not illicit hard drugs! Controlled substances? No! The friend who smuggled them explained that she'd offered one to Melissa but didn't actually believe my wife would take one. Melissa did, though. Took a whole gummy bear. Even the friend who'd brought them rarely took a full one.

Okay, I thought, *my wife is going to, at best, be high out of her mind and, at worst, overdose on one weed-infused gummy bear.* So what do I do, being the good husband that I am? I take one with her. Whatever happens to her will happen to me. In sickness and in health, till death do us part. We are both drug addicts now.

Except, as with all good edible stories, nothing happens right away. We finish eating our little appetizers and go back to the room to get ready for dinner. We shower, change clothes, and meet our friends at the van that will take us to the restaurant. Still, nothing has happened. We get to the restaurant after about a thirty-minute ride and sit down to order. It's been close to three hours now, and I've low-key forgotten we had even taken an edible. *Must have been weak,* I thought. We order our appetizers and a cocktail. Eat them. Still nothing. We order our main courses. And we are having great conversation when Lissa says, "My nose is clenched."

"What do you mean?" I ask.

"My nose is clenched. Look."

She scrunches her nose kinda like Barbara Eden in *I Dream of Jeannie.* Or Elizabeth Montgomery in *Bewitched.* Whichever one it is, you know what I'm talking about.

"My nose is clenched, Kev. Feel it."

I touch the bridge of her nose. Of course, it doesn't feel like anything unusual, but she is convinced her nose is clenched. She repeats this to the table. Everyone sitting around knows exactly what is happening—except me, because this is the first time that we've used hard drugs. (Okay, the second . . .)

"My nose is clenched, Kev! You're not feeling it."

I don't know what to tell her. She's never acted like this. I can't tell if she's playing. She takes a sip of her drink and it hits her.

"Whoaaaa!"

She looks like she's just ridden a merry-go-round at warp speed.

"I think it just hit me," she says.

Then it dawns on me. *Oh, that's right, we've taken drugs! That's probably why her nose feels clenched!*

"I've got to go to the bathroom and wash my face," says Melissa.

She hops up and scurries to the restroom, which is not far away. (See, the word *scurries* is funny.)

"Hurry back," I call out. Then I start to laugh and sip my water, knowing water won't enhance anything.

A few minutes pass and she's still gone. I'm starting to wonder why she hasn't made it back to the table yet.

The drug-smuggling friend who brought the gummies says, "Hey, Kev, she's been gone a while. You should go check on her."

So I stand up—and that's when it hits me. As I rise, I feel like I'm working against the gravitational pull of Mars. Mind you, I have no idea what the gravitational pull of Mars is—but I imagine it's stronger than ours on Earth. And right now, Mars's gravity is holding me hostage. With each step forward, the world feels heavier and heavier. Finally, I make it to the bathroom and wait. Nobody goes in or comes out. A couple minutes pass, and a woman goes into the bathroom and comes out. She leaves the door open long enough for me to have a look. I don't see anyone under the stalls. Nobody is at the sink washing their hands.

She's been kidnapped! I think loudly. In my weed-addled mind, I'm at the beginning of the movie *Taken*. But I am not Liam Neeson, so if I don't find my wife, she will just be Took. I rush into the bathroom to be certain she's not there. She's not. I come out of the bathroom and, space boots still weighing me down, run toward the restaurant entrance. Mars's gravity fights me, but I'm determined. I race to the parking lot, but I don't see her.

I am running toward the street when a janitor yells out to me, "The van!"

I whip my head around to him, fully expecting to see my loving wife wearing a black sack over her head as she's being thrown into a white kidnapper van. Then I realize he's pointing at the van we came to the restaurant in. I turn around and run as fast as I can (which is not fast at all but feels fast to me) to get to the van. I slide the door open, and there she is lying on the first row of seats.

"I am not high, Kevin," she blurts out before I can say anything. Then she bursts into laughter. "You are just making me laugh because you are asking me things that I already know are true." She says this verbatim. (I know because, even through the fog of my weed high, I managed to record this hilarious episode on my phone. And, of course, I still have the video.)

Somehow her sentence makes sense to me because, well, we are both high. One of our friends comes over and startles me when he asks if I'm okay. Based on the stories I heard later, I must've looked very obviously high, but at the moment, I'm assuring him that I am fine and Melissa just needs to lie down. (I found out later that I was speaking as if words were coming out of my mouth for the first time.) I don't know how long it took, but we make it back to our hotel with two to-go bags full of lamb chops, mashed potatoes, vegetables, and bread. I set the bags on the table. We decide that it's best to just sleep it off. So we lie down.

Have you seen that scene in *Doctor Strange* when someone punches his soul out of his body? *That's* how high I feel. As I lie down on the bed, I can feel my body on the bed and my soul adrift in space. I'm ghost dad.

Eventually hunger reunites my body and soul, and together they float over to the table with our leftovers. I feel like I could eat a pillow, but I settle for the lamb chops. The chops are better than sex, at least for that night. The flavor is full. I'm ravenous. To this day, I've never tasted food that good, not before then or after. I put the bag back on the table and float back to the bed. I sleep for what feels like twenty-seven hours—and am startled awake by the sound of a loud crash.

"Somebody is in the room!" my wife says. Great. Now I am going to have to fight an intruder, and I still don't have Liam Neeson's skills. I look around in the darkness. There's another crashing sound. Suddenly, I realize I'd only drifted off for a few seconds and that I'd put my bag of food so close to the edge of the table that it'd fallen off. I am high as a kite. We sleep for what feels like another twenty-eight hours before we wake up sober.

Neither of us have had a smoke or bite of the devil's weed since.

Honestly, the lesson here is simple: Not everything is for social media. By the time you read this book, both experiences will be many years behind me. And as funny as I think my weed experimentation is, I've never told this story online. For a long time anyway, those experiences were reserved for my wife and close friends. I don't put all my business in Instagram and Twitter streets. I believe that some parts of you need to be saved for close friends, some other parts for you alone. Sure, I'm adding it now because it's a good story—but this still technically isn't on social media. It's just a little something for people who buy this book.

DON'T CHANGE FOR SUCCESS

As I've said, I never stopped doing my own thing, even when I was at All Def. My association with Russell's digital platform may have raised my profile higher than it'd ever been, but I remained an entrepreneur at heart. All Def was more tolerable than a bank, for sure. That wasn't because I'd suddenly learned to appreciate working for others. Rather, it was because, while a gig like AwesomenessTV was only contract work, All Def was now paying me an actual full-time salary to build networks and get a crash course in digital content creation and marketing—all while allowing me to continue to cultivate my own comedy sets and material. I continued flying out to do shows around the country, booking more gigs than ever before. What I didn't realize, though, was that my success had also left me vulnerable in some ways, especially to the opinions of others.

See, prior to All Def, I was happy to wing it as a comedian. In Tacoma, I had developed a style and a topical focus that had won me a sizable group of supporters. (Remember, I was the guy who used to pour water on himself while mocking an R&B singer performing gospel.) But now that I was in Los Angeles and getting more notice, I found my comedy being scrutinized more closely than ever. Suddenly, I had critics who were telling me stuff like I used music too much to be a "real" comedian and that I wasn't funny unless I talked about church.

I decided to prove them wrong. One year, I vowed to not have any music or church material in my act. I spent that entire stretch doing secular humor and working without the live band that I'd made a staple of my shows since my early days working with Nate Jackson.

I pulled it off—but I was miserable. It's kind of like LeBron James when he was playing that heel role because people were mad at him from his time with the Miami Heat. LeBron was like, *I'm going to be a villain,* but it wasn't really his natural disposition. Same thing with me. Sure, I could do stand-up without jokes about being a Christian or without a band delivering a driving beat. But why should I? That's not who I am. I needed to get back to being me, to how I did comedy back when I was playing churches. Once I did, I was comfortable again, happy even.

It's commonly said that success changes us. But the truth is, we too often choose to change ourselves for success. And sometimes, that can be a surefire way to set yourself up for more failure.

THE END OF THE BEGINNING

Over the four years I worked at All Def Digital, my teammates and I did a lot of work, some of which made me shake my head in shame, much of which I remain proud of to this day. We encountered a lot of doubt about the viability of the platform and won over our share of skeptics. We survived a turbulent digital landscape, bad hires, heated criticism of our early content, and a ruthless office culture.

We could not, however, survive Russell Simmons.

In 2017, Russell was hit with two devastating charges of sexual misconduct. The first allegation, from model Keri Claussen Khalighi, claimed that in the 1990s Russell made aggressive advances toward her, forced her to perform oral sex on him in front of a Hollywood director, and penetrated her in a shower. She was seventeen at the time. Only eleven days later, a second charge was leveled by former actress Jenny Lumet. In a newspaper column, she said that when she was twenty-four, Russell drove her to his home and forced her to have sex with him. The following year saw more allegations of sexual assault directed against Russell, and allegations have continued to pile up ever since. One of the women he's accused of assaulting even served Russell a defamation lawsuit in Bali, where he moved, some say, to escape the charges against him. (Russell has denied all the allegations.)

When the first charge dropped, we knew almost right away that it was over for us. That same day, Russell announced that he was stepping away from all his ventures. With him went our chief pipeline for funding. Suddenly, after years of sacrifices and hard work, we were broke, dispirited, and anxious about the future. Whatever momentum we'd built when I first arrived had evaporated in the heat of Russell's controversies. Employees throughout the company started drafting plans to escape.

I ran toward my jokes. In 2018, I got booked to go on my first national comedy tour, which forced me to spend a portion of whatever time I had left at All Def working remotely. I'd be in the office the first four days of the week, but come Thursday night, I was jumping on a flight to whatever destination my next gig was in. Fridays I would work remote, answering texts and emails, giving notes on sketches and sharing ideas over the phone. And then I would spend that weekend performing as much as I could before flying back to LA for work. I did this for nearly the whole year. Meanwhile, in the office, an already toxic work culture had grown far worse. We were laying off people by the truckload. Nobody was happy. Our work began to suffer. The writing on the wall might as well have been scribbled in giant neon letters.

It didn't take long before I grew tired of the travel routine and, even more, the tension. I loved my job, and if there had been a way to stay, I would have. But the truth is, All Def was a zombie company at this point—technically still alive, but dead in every way that really counted. I didn't want to wait around to get laid off. I'd saved some money from work and the tour. Our family was doing fine.

My tour was going great. For the first time in my life, I was positioned to quit a job without throwing my family's life into disarray. *I guess this is my cue,* I told myself. Near the end of 2018, I quit All Def and went out on my own. That would mark the last time I ever worked a regular job.

In the years since the Russell Simmons debacle, All Def has rebounded to a degree. The rapper T.I. backed a group, Culture Genesis, that bought the company in 2019. Since then, they've developed some new talent as well as a little of the old. My friend Patrick Cloud, who worked under me as an intern when he first started, is still there. He runs content now and is probably one of the most talented creatives in digital media, especially when it comes to Black content. Other members of our old team have gone on to do big things in their own right. In fact, in my eyes, the best thing about All Def was the opportunity it created for so many of the people who worked there.

But as much as the platform helped others, I probably benefited more.

My channel and my reputation both got huge boosts from my association with All Def and the amazing litany of comedians who came through there. I still get recognized from many of those shows, even though I haven't been on All Def in years. *Great Taste* has become a lot of people's "comfort show." It has millions of views. Fans talk about it the same way other people talk about *The Office* or *Martin*. Matter of fact, my son loves *Great Taste,* and he still watches it.

And it's this last point that may mean the most to me. That's because, even in light of some of my biggest accomplishments, my kids tend to be some of my most pointed critics. I'm not a failure in their eyes, but, as little kids, they weren't exactly wowed by my successes or my struggles.

Take, for example, the time I sat down and recorded a heartfelt talk with Isaiah about all of my lifelong dreams.

Son: You wanted to be a YouTuber-slash-social-media-comedian?

Me: Nooo . . . Interestingly enough, I thought I was going to go to the NBA.

Son: Hahahahahahahaha!

(Pause. Silence.)

Me: Heh.

Son: You're not kidding?? I thought you were just being funny!

Me: No . . . Heh.

Son: You really thought you were going to the NBA?

Me: That *was*, like, my dream. As you laugh in my face, I realize I . . .

I just left the conversation where it was. There wasn't much more I could add. Like I said, unimpressed. Not only that, but, as you can see, my boys also are more than ready to mock me endlessly if the occasion demands. So, to have created something at All Def that my boys actually cherish and fondly remember?

That may be my greatest success of all.

PART FOUR

Falling Forward

TOUR DE FORCE

By now, you've figured out that there has been a definite pattern to my journey. I'd grind my butt off and reach a point where I thought I had finally neared the promised land, only to see my dream crash and burn yet again. The Bay Area Black Comedy Competition was going to make me the next Jamie Foxx—until I bombed so badly that I nearly quit stand-up altogether. The deal with AwesomenessTV was going to turn me into a successful screenwriter and my sons into internationally renowned media darlings—until the bosses refused to renew our contract. All Def Digital was going to make me a YouTube superstar—until Russell Simmons's legal troubles sent us into a death spiral. Stardom—and more important, the freedom to do my own thing without restriction—always seemed to be one break away, but that was the one break I could never catch.

The one silver lining in all those failures is that, somehow, they often led to even better, more lucrative opportunities. Now, just as I'd been blessed to go from Nate Jackson's comedy night to AwesomenessTV to All Def, another opportunity opened up even as All Def unraveled. In 2018, I got booked on the Like, Share, Tag tour, my first national tour. The tour featured a number of comedians who, like me, had found popularity on social media and whose comedy was grounded in church experiences. The Lord had literally given me—us—an opportunity.

Growing up, I'd never even considered the notion of a Christian comedian. Suddenly, I was being paid to travel the country with a whole group of 'em! It was a great ensemble, too: Christi Lockett, who'd blown up on YouTube by way of a character she created named Miss Shirleen; my good friend Anna Douglas, a brilliant young gospel comedian from North Carolina; my man Karlton Humes, a hilarious brother who goes by the stage name NotKarltonBanks; and myself.

We had a blast. The venues—we played everywhere from churches to concert halls—were often packed. Our audiences were usually energetic and eager to laugh. Night in, night out, we got golden opportunities to not just strut our best material but also push our social media platforms and get more eyes on our channels. And yeah, we were making a little bit of money, too.

The way it worked was, our promoter would find a venue, cover the cost of the location, and then split half the ticket sale proceeds with me, Christi, Anna, and Karlton. He'd also cover the cost of our flights and our hotels. Because he was taking all the upfront risk, we didn't have to worry about losing money if we didn't sell tickets. He ate that cost. He also made sure that we had dinner before every show. We could go to someplace in the church and they'd have baked chicken or burgers or whatever to make sure we were taken care of. Everything was going great.

Things went so well, in fact, that two months into my first tour ever, I quit so I could start my own.

It went down just before the Texas leg of our tour. We were scheduled to do a three-day weekend in Dallas, Houston, and San Antonio, but, for whatever reason, tickets to the San Antonio show were not moving. (Honestly, no matter what I do, I've never sold well in San Antonio, even to this day. Don't ask me why. You'd think that since I was born and raised in El Paso, I might have better luck in another Texas city. Nope.) The Dallas and Houston shows were selling well, but San Antonio was not interested. So the promoter comes to the comedians with an offer.

"Yo, if we can push the San Antonio sales to the point where Houston and Dallas are, we have a chance to make more than we've ever made on the tour," he told us. "Y'all might be able to make ten grand a person if we do this right."

Ten grand? Each? We already were getting what I *thought* was good money for the tour, earning as much as $6,000 per weekend. Plus, the promoter was covering all the risk. I thought things were as good as they were going to get. But ten grand per person? That was crazy!

Or was it?

If this was a cartoon, a light bulb would've appeared over my head in that moment. For the first time, I got a sense of just how lucrative a tour could be. Up until then, I'd been so content with the money I was earning as talent that I'd never stopped to consider what the promoter was making off us. I mean, we already were promoting the show online and then being forced to give up half of the money made at the door. And even though not every venue was huge, many of the cities where we were selling out had venues that could hold anywhere from fifteen hundred to two thousand people. You only had to sell a fraction of that many tickets to make a profit, especially if you were receiving 100 percent of the door.

Right then, I knew that my time had come. I'd spent years humping in nine-to-five purgatory—and, after that, years struggling to please mercurial leaders at AwesomenessTV and All Def. Now I saw a chance to follow through on the only dream I'd ever really harbored, the dream of being my own boss. It was the dream that had gotten me fired from KeyBank, that had spurred me to leave Tacoma for LA, that had kept me motivated even when nothing around me was going as planned. If I could make touring work, I thought, I'd never have to work for anyone else ever again. I decided to take a chance on myself.

I went to the promoter not long after and quit the tour. It wasn't that he was shady or incompetent. He was a good guy who just had the misfortune of being in the way of my lifelong dream.

"I'm sorry," I explained to him, "but staying on is just not good business."

And with that, I went out on my own. I left the tour, wrapped up my work at All Def over the next several months, and stayed out on the road working for myself with a team I put together. Since then, I've never had to split my money with another promoter, never had to report to another boss, and never had to fork over my talent and time to anyone else's company.

Best of all, I've never looked back.

Of course, facing forward didn't mean that there weren't still potholes and hurdles in the road ahead. Being in the driver's seat only meant that I was now most responsible for steering around them.

THE REAL COMEDIANS
OF SOCIAL MEDIA

After leaving the Like, Share, Tag tour, I immediately got started putting together my own bill. One of my first ideas was to incorporate some of the content that I did on my YouTube channel into a live show. That included segments like *The Love Hour,* an hour-long podcast about relationships that I hosted with Melissa. I knew that could succeed because my wife and I have always been able to take a lot of the same honesty and humor that make our marriage work and translate them to the social media stage. Melissa's not only insightful, but she's also a lot funnier than many people suspect.

People would want to hear good old-fashioned stand-up comedy, too—which meant I'd need to find other comics who could make the jump from social media to a live comedy stage without losing a step. For my first pick, I turned to my friend Tahir Moore, a funny and creative dude who'd helped drive some of our funniest-ever sketches while working at All Def. Not only was he hilarious, he and I had great chemistry. He also had real stand-up experience.

There was only one minor complication: I'd had to fire Tahir several months before.

Things at All Def had been going terribly. Russell was out. The brand was losing value. Money was drying up. Everyone was stressed beyond belief. We were going through layoffs and restructuring every three months. It seemed like every week, I or one of the other division leaders was being asked to let a staff member go.

One Monday, the powers that be called me into an office and told me point-blank that I was going to have to lay off a certain number of people that week. At the time, Tahir was working with Megan Thomas Williams on a show that, as funny as it was, was also very expensive for All Def to produce. I was told I'd have to cut the show itself but that we'd transfer Tahir and Meg to another project so they could stay on payroll. *All right, cool.*

I even remember double-checking with the C-suite executive, just to make sure. We'd had two or three rounds of layoffs by that point, so everybody was antsy, trying to decide if they should ride out the tough times or look for work elsewhere. Tahir and Meg deserved to know their fates.

"Am I going to have to let them go?" I asked. "Because if I'm going to have to let them go, tell me now so I don't get their hopes up. Shoot straight with me so I can shoot straight with my team."

"No," the executive assured me, "Tahir and Meg are going to be fine. If we can get his show off the books, we can still keep them on salary. We can justify their cost in other ways."

"Y'all sure?"

"Yes, Kevin. They'll be fine."

So I call in Tahir and Meg and repeat what they've told me.

"This show is going to be dropped, but your jobs are safe," I tell them. "We're going to move you here and here, blah, blah, blah, blah, blah."

They handled the news like professionals. It didn't matter what moves the company made as long as their jobs were safe. The same thinking was pretty much true of all of us.

Then Friday comes. Another meeting in the C-suite. Another directive.

"You're going to have to lay off ten more people," my boss told me.

When I ask who has to go, he starts listing people. Then he names Tahir. My anger and frustration erupted before I could catch myself.

"Yo, I just asked you if this was gonna happen!" I reminded him.

His answer? "Yeah, yeah, we know, but we crunched the numbers again. We're going to have to let 'em go."

I knew the decision wasn't mine, but it still felt like my fault. Department leaders at All Def had all become the grim reapers for our divisions. We were slashing budgets and letting people go company-wide. But our comedy department was the heart and soul of the company, so when we had to lay off talent, it always seemed to hit differently. (Of course, I'm sure the folks in sales and marketing felt the same way.) Further complicating the situation was the fact that the people I was laying off weren't just co-workers, they were also my friends. So yeah, I was feeling pretty terrible.

Unsurprisingly, although he understood the situation, Tahir didn't make it any better. Even today, he gleefully jokes to people about how "Kev fired me." Truth is, because he's so talented, we found ways to keep Tahir involved. He kept working for the company as a freelance writer, and he wound up making more money than he did as a full-time employee. He was invoicing for everything. We just didn't keep him on salary.

Of course, whenever he's trying to cast me as the villain, Tahir never tells the part about how he made more money after he was let go. He'd rather stick with that scurrilous lie! But since this is my book, I'm going to tell the whole truth! Y'all, don't be listening to Tahir!

———

The other comedian I went and got was my friend Tony Baker. Why? Because I wanted the show to be good, and Tony, simply, was the best comedian I knew. Incredibly talented brother. Even to this day, I think Tony Baker is better than me. (So does my son, but we'll get into that later.) Here's how good Tony is: When I was putting together the lineup for the show, I had people coming to me urging me to leave Tony off. Apparently, the rule of comedy tours is that if you're the headliner, you never get someone who is funnier, or even *almost* funnier, than you. When you go onstage, the audience is supposed to be like, "Oh, the real comic is here now."

But remember, before I was doing stand-up, I was writing and producing plays. Coming from the world of theater, I knew that when you're putting on a show, your job is to put on the best performance you possibly can. It never crossed my mind to pick people I didn't think were funny. My job is to bring the funny, and if they're better than me, then they're going to inspire me to be better. I'm not going to be like, *Oh, lemme pick No Jokes McGee so he can lowkey bomb every night!* Nah, bring my level up.

I had befriended Tony years before precisely because I was so impressed with his humor and stage presence.

I remember the first joke I ever heard him tell, at the Nate Jackson Super Funny Comedy Show. He came on stage and told the crowd that he was terrified of clowns. The audience started cracking up. Then he went on to say, "I know you don't think clowns are scary, but say it's late and you get into an elevator and there is just a single clown in there. Are you getting on that elevator?" The audience cracks up and says collectively, "Noooo."

The joke was so funny and memorable that, as one of my first official duties at All Def, I wound up writing a sketch for him and Spoken Reasons based on that clown premise. In the years since, of course, Tony has won over millions of followers on social media with his voiceovers of animal clips and his overall hilarity. Back then, not nearly as many people had heard of him, but I knew right away that he was funny.

There wasn't much else to it: I was a super fan of his comedy and just decided one day, *I'm gonna be his friend!* So I reached out and we just hit it off. Then, while I was still living in Tacoma, I met him in person one night at Nate's. Our friendship has been a close one ever since.

When I began working for Russell Simmons, Tony was one of the first people I reached out to about doing work for us. In addition to the clown skit, we created a weekly sports show for him called *Two Minute Drill*. I think we were giving him something like $200 to write a skit and $50 to act in it. I know, Tony was worth way more, but he was still appreciative. He used to tell me, "Brother, you kept the bill paid with that show!" It reminded me a lot of the gratitude and pride I felt each time I made even a pittance from one of my little coffee shop gigs. And it also meant we hired him a lot. *Get Tony Baker for this. Get Tony Baker for that.*

No way I wasn't gonna get Tony Baker when it came time to put together my own tour.

I decided to call the tour the Real Comedians of Social Media Tour as a play on the TV show *Real Housewives of Atlanta.* I thought it was a cool name. Apparently, it came as a shock to some because, believe it or not, a lot of people didn't know I performed stand-up comedy. My YouTube channel and my work at All Def had brought me a significant audience by this point, but much of that audience had no idea that I was more than a skit guy. In addition, other people were upset by the name. They suggested that I was throwing subliminal shots at people who weren't on the tour. *Kev is trying to say we not real comedians!* That wasn't the case. Honestly, I just thought the name was funny, given the spate of reality shows with similar names.

Anyway, I named the show, negotiated a set performance fee with Tahir and Tony, and then I went about trying to line up venues. As you might figure, even if you haven't ever promoted a show, booking venues can be demanding and expensive. Many places want a certain amount of money up front and/or a cut of the door. Sometimes, they ask you to do meet and greets ahead of performances. You have to make sure they have the equipment and space to accommodate you. And most of all, if you're still up-and-coming like we were, you have to find inducements to get butts in seats.

Even from my days working at the bank, I've always excelled at selling people on incentives. In some ways, getting people to buy a ticket to my comedy show wasn't much different than convincing them to apply for a credit card. I knew it was all about the perks. To get folks to come out to a venue even before I'd booked it, I came up with an idea: If I was doing a show in, say, Los Angeles, I told people that if the venue was within an hour of your city and you bought your tickets early, they would cost $15—which was 50 percent off the full price. I put all the tickets on sale on the same day for each city on our itinerary, which covered as many as forty different locations.

It was a crazy act of faith, as I had no idea whatsoever whether my plan would work—until it did. Within an hour of me posting the ticket offers online, fans all over the country started flooding the digital box office. We were selling in Illinois, California, Texas, Florida, you name it. On the first day, I earned more than $15,000 in ticket sales in barely an hour!

You gotta remember, for me, the benchmark for a great salary was still the $35,000 I earned when I worked for Bank of America. That was my idea of good money back then. But now, staring at the computer screen as those day one ticket sale tallies steadily ticked up, I knew that everything that I'd believed about myself and my ability was coming true. I'd earned in fifteen minutes what it used to take me half a year to make. Believing in your talent is one thing. To see it happen right in front of your eyes?

That was the moment I *knew* that I'd gambled on myself, and, finally, I'd won big.

THE WAFFLE HOUSE DEAL
THAT WASN'T

Launching the tour was a risk, yes, but it was a calculated one. I couldn't know for sure that we'd put fans in seats until the ticket sales started rising, but I had good reason to suspect that a bet on myself would pay off.

I'd come a long way from the days when my own kid got more views than I did. By the time I decided to tour, I'd gone from a few thousand followers to seven hundred thousand on Facebook alone. I had built a following there by simply posting my YouTube videos. Native video was relatively new to Facebook back then. Since more people hung out there than on YouTube, the content I shared became hugely successful because it was stuff that was rarely, if ever, seen. Suddenly, between Facebook, Twitter, and Instagram, KevOnStage literally had *millions* of followers. *If I can't tour with seven hundred thousand Facebook followers, when can I?* I thought. But as nice a surprise as my growing numbers were, I was even more stunned, and happy, to learn that corporate America was paying attention, too.

I found this out not long before the tour, when a short video I did joking about Waffle House—how it's not clean and why the people who love to eat there don't care—began doing jaw-dropping numbers online. To date, it's earned forty-nine million views on Facebook alone. That's not even counting the number of times it's been ripped and reposted on Facebook, let alone its popularity on other digital platforms. It's the most universally loved video I've ever made, by a wide margin. What's even funnier to me is that I hardly thought about it before making it. I'd read an article on Twitter from the *Atlanta Journal-Constitution* about Waffle House failing health inspections. I had recently done a bit in Fayetteville, North Carolina, about Waffle House, and it absolutely crushed. The joke wasn't even supposed to be part of my set. It was just an offhand observation that I came up with on the spot. But it worked great.

As I'd point out on stage, Waffle House floors are always sticky. The tables are small. They bring the food out to your table as it's ready, one plate at a time . . . even though the tables are small. The silverware is dirty. One time, when I brought this fact to my server's attention, he brought me a cup of hot water and stuck the silverware in the cup. I guess that was the solution. And I accepted it. I accepted it because the food is good and cheap. One time I saw a chef mixing my eggs with his hands—and I still ate it. And so what if Melissa and I watched a massive brawl erupt at a Waffle House in Dallas that ended with twelve people getting arrested while my wife and I never even got out of our seats? *This* was the Waffle House we knew. *This* was the Waffle House we loved.

Funny thing about that bit was, the *only* thing I exaggerated was the part about the chef cooking my eggs with his hands. The rest was cold, hard Waffle House truth. For the video, I just repeated the talking points from the stage. Next thing I know, it's on blogs and in newspaper articles, and I'm being asked to do interviews. It was crazy!

Then it got much crazier: I actually got hit up on email by the head of marketing at Waffle House, who wanted to know when I'd be in Atlanta next so they could thank me in person for giving attention to their brand and talk to me about other marketing opportunities. I could hardly believe it. I leaped at the offer.

"It just so happens," I told them in my immediate reply, "that I will be in Atlanta next week, and I would love to talk!"

Okay, so this wasn't technically true, at least not yet. I had absolutely no plans whatsoever to be in Atlanta—but I smelled money on the table. *I'm gonna get the biggest brand deal in my life!*

The synergy seemed so perfect. I had talked about their company in a funny way, and they loved it. So I immediately bought a ticket and began planning my trip to Atlanta. I spent $1,500 on the trip. Could I afford it? Not at all. I was popular online, but money was still an issue. Still, that didn't matter at that moment. *I'm gonna get a brand endorsement that will earn that fifteen hunna back in no time!* By my own math, this brand deal would certainly be worth at least $250K—please don't ask me how I settled on these numbers, because I have no idea. Anyway, $1,500 for plane fare and a hotel room was a mere drop in the bucket.

So I fly to Atlanta, grab a room at a hotel near the airport and meet the marketing executive . . . at a Waffle House restaurant. Not the corporate office, but a roadside location in some obscure section of the city. Should this have been a screaming red flag? Of course. Did I see it that way? Not at all.

As soon as I sat down, the marketing guy shook my hand and thanked me for stopping by while I was in town. He still had no idea that I'd flown out just to meet with them, and there was no way I was going to let on that this trip was strictly about landing my official Waffle House brand partnership. I nodded and smiled. He continued.

"I want to tell you up front that we don't do any sort of official brand partnerships. If you notice, we don't even do TV commercials. The most we have is billboards."

No, I had not noticed. I guess I should have, but I hadn't.

"We don't do franchises unless you work in-store," he went on. "Snoop Dogg asked to do a Waffle House franchise in LA. We turned him down."

I'm pretty sure my jaw literally dropped. I know for sure that at least my mouth was agape.

Y'all turned down Snoop?! Snoop D-O-Double-G?!

It was at this moment that I realized I had messed up. If they had turned down Snoop, then little ol' me had most certainly wasted a plane ticket.

"We just wanted to thank you for your hard work and posting that video," the executive said. "Here's a $250 gift card."

Two hundred and fifty American dollars. Actually, no, not even that—two hundred and fifty *Waffle House* dollars. To a Waffle House fanatic, that's equal to something like $19,000 in real money. But still, it was a far cry from the $250K I had decided earlier that Waffle House was about to pay me. Oh, and they also gave me a name tag.

Before we wrapped up our meeting, I asked if I could make a video in the kitchen. They were nice enough to agree. So I go back to the kitchen, and the staff taught me all the Waffle House lingo. "Pull one bacon" means prepare one side order of bacon. "Drop one hash brown" means get a hash brown order ready. "Mark" meant the end of an order. So I pulled all that jargon together in my skit, made the video, and took my Black behind back to LA.

At least I left with that gift card—and, man, did that come in handy. When the first tour kicked off, we wielded that gift card like it was a platinum Amex. That card fed us many a night and never ran out. Allow me to put my preacher hat on as I extol the virtues of that card. (Back me up with a Hammond organ in your mind, if you will.) *Every time we needed it, it was right there! Every swipe, it was right there! In the midnight hour when we were hungry, saints, it was there! Amen? Amen.* It reminded me of the Bible story where the prophet Elijah blesses a widow woman with oil and flour that never run out. That Waffle House card *never* stopped working, even after we had spent well over $250. Matter of fact, the only reason I'm not using it to this day is because I lost it.

So, in a way, I guess I did get my $1,500 back in pancakes and bacon. But the next time someone asks me about coming to town, I'll wait until I really do have plans to be there.

BROTHER'S KEEPER

As excited as I was for the tour, I was grappling with a large measure of sadness, too. That's because, a couple of months before I'd decided to go out on my own, my brother, Jason, was diagnosed with a disease I'd never even heard of before—something called multiple myeloma. Essentially, multiple myeloma is a form of cancer in plasma cells that affects everything from your bone marrow to your kidneys to your body's ability to produce healthy red and white blood cells.

The crazy thing is, our family only learned of the disease because Jason got into a car accident. When doctors x-rayed him to make sure he hadn't broken anything, they discovered weakness in his bones, which they later realized was being caused by the cancer. Nobody knows how it happened. It's not like getting lung cancer from smoking or skin cancer from extended periods in the sun. My brother's disease seemed to come out of nowhere. They scheduled him for a bone marrow transplant as soon as they could get him in.

Jay was my business partner—basically my manager—from the very beginning of my career. He had been there for everything. All the poorly planned ideas. All the hilariously failed trips. The hit performances as well as the bombs. Jay negotiated contracts. He helped book shows. He looked out constantly for my next big chance. Now, finally, after years of struggle, I was set to blow up on a fifty-city nationwide tour, something we'd always dreamed of doing together, and he wouldn't be there at all.

At the outset, his doctors prepped our family for the worst.

"People don't usually fully recover from this, ever," one of his doctors explained during one of our visits. "And even if it seems to go into remission, it doesn't really. You can get close to what may look like remission, but it'll still be there. People don't usually live more than five to seven years after a diagnosis."

As he spoke, I realized that I was struggling to comprehend what he was saying. I understood the words coming out of his mouth, but each one seemed to fly at me randomly, incoherent and unconnected to the words spoken before or after. My mind was shutting down. It refused to process this craziness. (If I'm being brutally honest with myself about it, I haven't fully processed it to this day.)

Then the doctor showed us Jason's X-rays, and I grew even more terrified. There were dark spots all over the images. The doctor called them "lesions," but actually, they were holes. In his bones. Man, that was heartbreaking.

From that day on, I lived every day with an almost suffocating fear for my brother's future. Immediately after his diagnosis, I held out hope that there might still be some slim chance he could make the tour, but it didn't take long for that hope to evaporate. Even though he'd eventually get the transplant he needed, multiple myeloma ravaged Jay's body. He was super weak all the time. He lost weight and height. At 6'1", 270 pounds, I'd always been bigger than him, but it wasn't like he was some puny dude. Jay was 5'11", about 190 at his peak. But as the cancer took its toll, I watched his body shrivel to the point where he stood about 5'9" and weighed less than 160 pounds.

Months after his diagnosis, the tour kicked off. While I traveled coast to coast, my brother was moving back in with our parents—who lived in North Carolina at this point—so he could go to Duke Medical Center for cancer treatment. The tour worked out amazingly. We were doing sold-out shows almost everywhere we performed. Tahir and Tony killed as much as I did. My name, my following, and my reputation had never been bigger. But my fear for Jason loomed over everything.

I'd dealt with death before. My grandmother had passed of old age. My uncle Rudy died in his early sixties, which was young still, but not uncommon. The idea of losing my brother, though? To cancer? In his forties? Make that make sense.

Yes, I was at what was then the pinnacle of my career—but success had never tasted so bittersweet.

NFL

With the popularity of the Real Comedians tour came significant growth in my social media audience. Over the next several months, one million followers became two million. Two million would eventually rise to three million. And with each increase came even more attention, not just from fans and other content creators but from more brands as well. Maybe Waffle House wasn't ready to have KevOnStage as an official ambassador—I mean, if they turned down Snoop Dogg I guess there wasn't much chance for me—but, as I learned, a number of other brands were more than willing to take a chance on me. And really, why not? I was a Christian family man who'd worked his way up from nothing. My comedy was clean. I wasn't shrouded in controversy or scandal. And I was blessed to have won the ear of millions of everyday people. Given that, I can't say it was totally unexpected when brands like cable giant Spectrum and General Motors' OnStar came calling to offer me some of my earliest endorsements.

As grateful as I was for some of those first deals, I had made up my mind long ago that I would only do the sort of work that was right for me. I wouldn't do anything that went against my beliefs as a Christian. I wasn't going to endorse any product that I didn't really like or use. And I wasn't going to do brand content that would embarrass me, my family, or Black folks in general. I love making money and being able to provide for my wife and children, but not all money is good money. Sometimes you gotta say no.

Which doesn't mean it's always easy.

Take the National Football League. About five, six years ago, the NFL reached out to me about doing promotional work. Mind you, I love sports—and football in particular. Although I'd played basketball in AAU and in high school, football always has been my favorite sport to watch on TV. Around this time, though, the NFL was in the middle of blackballing former San Francisco 49ers quarterback Colin Kaepernick for having the audacity to quietly take a knee during the national anthem as a way of protesting police brutality against Black Americans. Kaepernick hadn't played since the 2016 season, and at this point, it was clear that the NFL had locked him out with no intention of bringing him back. That's how I saw it, and you weren't going to tell me anything different. And so, like a lot of other Black folks in 2018 and 2019, I was so pissed off at how they were treating that brother that I had decided to boycott the league. I wasn't watching any games. I wasn't buying any gear. I'd even canceled my NFL Sunday Ticket package.

I need you to understand that I don't join every boycott. I'm not the type of guy who is looking for stuff to go out and protest. When you've got a high profile or a little bit of celebrity, people want you to be involved in everything, but that just ain't me. If I'm not boycotting a product or service, I'm not going to tell you that I am. On the flip side, though, when I *do* tell you I'm doing something, it's because I'm doing it for real, especially if I make it public. And on this issue, I was loud and clear. I wanted nothing to do with the NFL until it worked out a deal with Kaepernick. (This was before he'd settled with the league.) It wasn't easy. I probably could've snuck and watched a game or two without anybody ever knowing. But Kaepernick deserved justice. It was more than worth it to sacrifice football if it meant backing him.

So of course, six weeks into my boycott, the NFL reached out to me about a brand deal.

And, I mean, they really tested my mettle. They offered to fly me to New York and put me up while we worked out the deal. And they were going to pay more than I had ever received for any brand deal at that point, somewhere in the low six figures. Granted, that may not be much for someone like LeBron James or Matthew McConaughey, but for Kevin Fredericks, it was as generous an offer as I could wish for. And it wasn't like I couldn't have used the cash. At that point, I had far more popularity than money, and our bill collectors weren't in the habit of accepting celebrity as a form of payment.

Oh my God, I remember thinking. *They're really going to test me to see if I'm a man of my word!*

I sat down to talk to Melissa about it. We weighed the pros and the cons, and I won't lie: The offer was tempting. But ultimately, I had to tell the league no. I felt like I couldn't accept that offer in good conscience. Sure, I might have been able to continue ignoring the games and refusing to buy league merchandise even after I had taken the deal, but I would know I'd sold out my principles. And since I'd gone public about supporting the boycott, everyone else would know it, too.

Shortly after I passed on the deal, the NFL reached out to another Black content creator who was as popular as I was. I don't know that he ever said he was boycotting or whatever, but he ended up doing the deal that they had offered me. And guess what? He got no blowback at all! Nobody said a word about it. I was like, *Dang, if I didn't stand on principle, I really could have done that brand deal!* I don't think anybody would've been mad, but that didn't really matter. All that counted was that I didn't feel good about it for myself. I've never regretted that choice. It marked the first time I'd ever stood on business where an endorsement was concerned. It wouldn't be the last.

JASON BOUNCES BACK

In 2019, we launched our second Real Comedians of Social Media Tour. Now that we had the experience of doing a tour for ourselves, my team and I were ready to make the sequel even better than the first go-round. As far as I was concerned, the second tour was guaranteed to be better than the first, for one simple reason: My brother was recovering from cancer.

Jason had gotten the bone marrow transplant that he needed, and he was slowly rounding back into form. He'd never regain the height that bone cancer had taken from him, but he had gotten most of his weight back and, along with it, much of his strength. His immune system had essentially been wiped out, which meant he had to repeat the vaccine regimens most of us get as kids. Otherwise, he was great. His spirits were soaring.

You need to know that when he wasn't battling a life-threatening disease, my brother was a genuinely funny dude. He could spin a story as deftly as any preacher or comedian or public speaker ever, capturing scenes and recounting dialogue like some 'hood version of Garrison Keillor. He'd occasionally hop on social media and share his funny tales with the world.

For instance, there was the time in 2015 when he decided to take to YouTube and tell everybody about a small run-in I had with a rather large gentleman one night at LA's famous Roscoe's House of Chicken 'N Waffles. Y'know what? Instead of trying to explain it to you in my words, I'm just going to allow you to read for yourself what that man said.

Let's turn the next several pages over to my brother for . . .

THE STORY OF KEVONSTAGE ALMOST GETTING BEAT UP AT ROSCOE'S

(as told by Jason Fredericks)

So, Roscoe's—for those that have been and those that haven't—is a sketchy place off rip. Okay, let's get that out the way. Roscoe's is a sketchy place, right? And this is what I mean: Roscoe's is like a franchise version of the hole-in-the-wall in the 'hood. First of all, they're selling chicken and waffles. I mean, if that ain't sketchy in the first place . . . You already know what time . . . They selling *chicken and waffles*! If that is not going to be a sketchy place—it's sketchy . . .

Anyway, all their restaurants look like they used to be something else. You know those restaurants that look like old Burger Kings and old McDonald's? You know when you walk in and be like "What did this used to be? Was it—was the swap meet here?"

They always got people selling stuff outside. You can get mixtapes outside. You can get candles, fancy creams, and lotions. They got the oil man out there. If you ever need body oil and you don't know where to get it, go to Roscoe's, any Roscoe's in LA. You can go in there, you can get anything you need. There's a guy in that parking lot selling suits, mixtapes, anything you need. DVDs, CDs—all of that stuff is there at Roscoe's. I'm setting the picture for you, then you can understand.

Rugs . . . Rugs! Cats be like, *"I got these rugs from Iraq!"*

"How did you get to Iraq?"

"Don't worry about how I got to Iraq—but they straight from Iraq and Kuwait. I got these Kuwaiti rugs. You can lay down. Your girl gonna love ya, boss! Try it for ya boy! Mess wit' ya boy one time!"

One time, somebody was *outside* of Roscoe's selling chicken and waffles. Outside of Roscoe's!

"Hey, man, I'm selling plates. Listen, I've got these for the five. You gon' go in and pay the twelve. Come on now. I know these is Eggo waffles, but it's still cool. Listen, dog . . ."

You dropping chicken right outside the Roscoe's. Come on, bro . . .

Roscoe's is *that* place. So if you can think about the characters *outside* of Roscoe's then you can understand the characters that are *inside* of the Roscoe's . . .

We didn't live in Cali, but when Michael Jackson died, he died on like a Thursday. We flew to Cali for some shows on Friday. Well, Michael Jackson died and when we landed in Cali the next day, they already were selling Michael Jackson shirts. They spelled Michael M-I-K-E-A-L-E, Mike-ale Jackson! *RIP Mikeale.* That's what they was selling. True story, man. Right in the front. "Ay, man, I got the Michael Jackson mixtape. I got the Michael Jackson—"

"What does the shirt say?"

"Oh, that says *Mikeale.* I know him."

That's what Roscoe's is about.

Everybody comes in there—pimps, players, hustlers, mack daddies, gangsters. Everybody comes in Roscoe's. White people come in Roscoe's because they think it's cool and then they go in there and be like, *"This is Roscoe's, little Jimmy. This is 'Roscoe's: We About That Life'—and we're trying to show you how we are **not** about that life. We are not about this life. But these chicken and these waffles? It is excellent. Your mom can't fry nothing. She keep putting Shake 'N Bake on her chicken. I'm gonna show you how these Black people do it cuz those Blacks at my work, they know how to do some food up . . ."*

Roscoe's: We about that life.

So let's get into the story.

I think that day it was me and Kev and Ant and Melissa and the boys. I don't think anybody else is there. And just real quick: Ant, he's our good friend. Ant's not our brother, but we're close, very, very close.

All right, so we're there eating. And if you know, it's Roscoe's so Kev always gets the Obama. Him and Lis, they always get the wings with the waffle. Ant always gets two waffles with the chicken. I always get the legs, okay?

So we're sitting down eating. So there's this Mexican guy and his girlfriend, sitting behind us. The Mexican guy, let's just say his name is Felipe. And the girl's name is Roxanne. So Felipe and Roxanne is sitting behind us. We had already ate; we were getting ready to leave. As we're getting ready to leave, we get up. I was sitting down, and Kev got up first. He was rushing to go pay.

If anybody ever been with Kevin anywhere, you know Kev always has his phone in his hand. He didn't have his phone in his hand yet, but he was reaching for his phone. So as he's reaching for his phone this is what happened:

His phone is in his pocket. He's walking by—it was the perfect storm—so he's walking by Felipe and Roxanne's table, all right, and he pulls out his phone.

Mind you, Kevin wants to wear jeans he shouldn't be wearing. Let's talk about that. Kevin has extra big thighs, and Kevin can't wear the jeans that normal men wear. He has to get his thighs cut out. Lissa gotta take his pants to the thigh people, and they gotta let his thighs out.

Just so happens, this time those jeans hadn't been let out yet. He wanted to look cool and wear his little pants so everybody can see his calf muscles. So everybody who wanted to see his calf muscles, we can see every muscle in his thigh. And so we saw all that.

He's walking, and his phone is in his pocket. He tried to pull out his phone from his pocket—but his thigh has it! He didn't realize his thigh was saying, *No, phone, come back here! You're not going anywhere! You're not taking this phone with you. This is my phone! You know why? Because you have choked us out in these pants that you should have let Lissa let out!*

Brothers, send your pants with your wife to get the thighs let out if you got extra thighs!

So he's pulling his phone out, okay? He's pulling his phone out. The thighs have the phone. He's trying to pull it out, so naturally the phone flies . . . in slow motion. *Pachoo choo choo—boom!*

I saw the phone flip around. The phone was looking like, *Oh no, no!*

It fell into Felipe's waffle and food that he just got.

The dude with the ankle bracelet had just brought Felipe and his girl his food. He knew Felipe from the pen.

"Hey, Felipe, I'm gonna go run back and get your food."

"All right! Thank you, *ese*. I appreciate it, bro . . . I'm glad to see you are doing good, bro!"

So the dude with the ankle bracelet—um, Jamal—brought Felipe his food. As soon as he did that, Felipe sat down. "Roxanne, baby, you know I love you, girl. You my baby, you know I love you. I'm gonna have two babies with you, okay. I didn't want to take you to the Mexican place. I wanted to bring you to where they're about that life!"

Then here comes the phone as soon as they bring the food, right into Felipe's food! I mean, hard.

You know when you drop your phone, and you think it cracked? That's how loud it was—*crack!* To where you'd be like, *No! I didn't buy the insurance!* That's how his phone fell.

Then Felipe, he looked up. You ever seen somebody transform into a different person when they stand up? *You weren't that person when you were sitting down! You were Felipe from the 'hood! And now you turned into Machete? Felipe to Machete?*

Let me try to describe him. He had veins in his arms like he was a Snickers bar. If The Rock was Mexican, it was him. Picture The Rock with a ponytail. It was this man! Picture all the wrestlers in the WWF. It was him! Have you ever seen somebody stand up, and they just keep going? Mexicans aren't even that tall in real life. He stood up, it was like he turned into the Shaq of Mexicans. I was like, *Mexican Shaq, dang!* He was taaaallllll.

When he stood up, the first thing Kev did was—*pffft.* He farted.

He farted because when Kevin gets nervous, he starts farting. Gas was everywhere. Have you ever started thinking like, *I wish I'd been working out.* I don't know if anybody's ever been in a fight, but if you're gonna fight, you get a little bit scared. You feel like, *Man, I don't really want to fight, but I gotta protect myself.* Have you ever been in that, that type of situation, where you have to fight, you gotta prove yourself, you gotta be ready—and you're not really ready?

It's just, it's just one of those things where life just taking over. He just started farting. Felipe stands up: *Rrrarrrr!* Kev: *Pfffffffftttttt.* "Lis, I'm sick . . ." That's what he does when Kev farts a lot: "Lis, I'm sick, I'm sorry."

So he automatically turned to her. "Lis, I'm sick, I'm sorry." We're all still looking up at Machete, and Kev is farting. Have you ever been about to fight somebody and wish you knew karate? Have you ever been about to fight somebody and it feel like in your arms, your strength isn't there? That's what the look on Kev's face was.

So Machete got up. "Hey, bro, what the hell, dude? I'm out here with my girl. What are you doing?"

And Kev's like, "Bro, it was an accident"—because, technically, he didn't know his thighs were gonna hold on to the phone. So he was like, "Listen, man, my thighs were holding on to the phone . . . I got big thighs, and I'm supposed to let these pants out but I couldn't . . . My wife . . . That's my wife over there . . . I was supposed to send these pants with my wife two weeks ago, and I didn't send them and so my thighs is upset so they have my . . . I was getting ready to go pay for my food, my family's food *and* your food because I saw you over here talking to Roxanne, and Roxanne, I mean, you look so beautiful, you're . . . I don't know why your eyeliner is all the way to your ear but you look fantastic, Roxanne . . ."

Machete's not happy.

"No, bro! How do you pull your phone out, how do your thighs hold your phone, *ese*? How do they do that?"

As I'm looking on, Big Brother wants to jump out. I'm looking on like, *Dang*. Ant is like, "Shoot," and starts looking down and tying his shoes.

"Ant, what are you doing?"

"I'm tying my shoes."

"You got sandals on, bro."

Machete's up now, because he's gotta prove his love to Roxanne. He's like, "How did it happen? How did it happen? How did it happen? How does that happen?"

And here goes Roxanne: "Yeah, how would your phone fall out of your pants like that and land automatically into Machete's plate? Felipe, babe, don't let him do that because you know what I'm saying, babe."

And we were like, "Roxanne, shut up with your stupid makeup on!"

There are a few moments in your life where you're like, *You know what? We might not make it out of here. God, this is what you have for us? This is the plan for our life? You brought the Play-makers to Roscoe's: About That Life so we can realize that we're not about that life? And we're gonna die today. Because there's no way as an older brother that I can let my younger brother get killed by Machete. And his family's there so I'm gonna have to die, too.*

All right, if this is your will, Lord, let your will be. If you want Machete to kill us, God, take over . . . Your will, Lord. Your will if you want to give us into the hands of the Machete-inites. Don't let it hurt, Lord. Let me go quick, Jesus.

It was faith over fear. We had faith that God was gonna take us through this battle, but fear was saying, *Lord, I don't know how we're gonna get through these Machete-inites.* But we was gonna stand up there as brothers.

Kevin held his arms up. I ran over and held his arms up, too, because the Bible says when they have the arms up they was gonna win the battle. Machete draws back. He was about to go in for the kill—but God said, "No, hold on." The Machete man pulled his hand back to strike him down—but God was there.

He sent security over! Somebody say, "Thank God for security!"

God had angels watching over me because he knew we was going to *Roscoe's: About That Life.* He knew the enemy was there before we got there. He knew Machete was taking Roxanne out. He knew Kev had sinned and didn't let his pants out before we got there. But when we got there, somebody said, "Jesus will meet you there!"

Security surrounded us and said, "Hold on, Machete! This is God's man here! We know his thighs were big! We know the thigh held on, but listen, don't you set your hand on him! Do you know that God will not allow the Machete-inites to lay a hand upon thee?"

The security came over and said, "I saw the whole thing and from my perspective . . . the thigh is what took this over. Blame it on the pants that was sewn too tight. Blame it on thighs, bayyy-bay!"

And that's when district elder Machete, leader of the Machete-inites, put his sword down and did pass brother Kevin out.

Perspective, saints.

We pray against all thighs right now, Father God. We pray against all thighs that are too big right now, even thighs that are at KFC and that're implanted with all these extra things, Lord, that are making the thighs too big. Chickens are suffering. Roosters are suffering. Birds all around the globe are suffering from too much thigh meat, Jesus. We ask you to cast it down, Lord. Give them regular feed. Give the humans regular feed so their thighs aren't so big no more, Lord. We thank you for the hedge of protection over the Machete-inites. We thank you . . .

So yeah, that's who my brother could be when he was feeling good and at his best. And now that he was healthier than he'd been in more than a year, Jay had decided he wanted to get back to being that guy, back to the life that he'd missed out on since his diagnosis in 2017. To my delight, he announced that he'd be joining us on the road as the tour manager.

Another thing he'd do once he got back to his old self was show up in town unannounced, just to surprise us. I can't count the number of times my kids would come downstairs and Jason would be there to surprise them. You know that phrase about somebody always lighting up a room? That was Jason. He had a presence that was like a cookie. You don't necessarily *need* a cookie, but you love them. And everybody is a little happier when there are cookies.

Jay wasn't just behind the scenes, either, not publicly or privately. Along with handling the tour, Jay could also be found near the entrances of our venues. He wasn't telling jokes or doing skits. Before each show, he'd be out there selling T-shirts that gave glory to God for his recovery. Each shirt was emblazoned with the words *I Have a Powerful Testimony*. And each show opened with Jay sharing that testimony to our audiences. I mean, he would give his *whole* testimony. He'd walk out on stage before any of us would perform, and he'd lay out his story, how good his life had been before the cancer diagnosis, how the news that he was sick had come out of nowhere. And he'd relate to the audience just how devastated he and our family were when the doctors issued what we all thought amounted to a death sentence.

"I had cancer," he'd start. "They told me I have this long to live. But, as of now, I am healed!" He'd remind them that, at the end of the day, God was in charge.

It was powerful, moving, and all true. By all appearances, he'd made his way back from what we'd thought was a certain death sentence. He was proud and grateful to have beaten that disease. Your heartstrings couldn't help but be pulled. He sold a lot of shirts, too.

The only drawback was that he was giving that testimony to open up a comedy show. As powerful as his words were, they didn't exactly set the table for those of us who had to follow him with jokes. One evening, Tahir, who usually was the first comic onstage, had to point this out: "Hey, I get it, man. Powerful testimony. But uh . . . you bring the room down. Then I have to come behind you and try to make people laugh? Brother, help me out here."

I had to laugh at Tahir's exasperation, even if it was true. Jay did bring the mood down a little bit. But what could we do? The man had gone through a hellish ordeal, and he was thankful that he was not only still alive but getting most of his health back, too. He still had to go in and have regular checkups and all that type of stuff, but there was never any indication that anything was wrong. Outside of being a little shorter than he used to be, he was in fantastic health and shape. He was his old self, funny, cracking jokes, traveling all over the world. Even toward the end of 2019 and the early part of 2020, when the COVID-19 pandemic was starting to take hold, he kept going. We'd be like, "Bro, you need to stop traveling so much, man. You got a weakened immune system."

And he was just like, "Bro, I'm living my life. I don't care."

He was traveling against doctor's orders, but nevertheless he stayed on the road. If he wasn't out with us, he was out watching his son play basketball in AAU tournaments or taking his wife on dates. You'd have no idea he'd spent the past year and a half fighting off a killer disease.

Seeing him like this began to ease my mind over time. The fear that had dominated my unoccupied moments in 2018 slowly began to recede. My brother was back.

DONALD TRUMP COST ME $50,000 . . . BUT IT WAS WORTH IT

I wish my second tour could've run through late 2020, but the coronavirus had other ideas. With the world sick and reeling, we had to pack it in for most of that year. We did manage to put together a virtual version of our tour, dubbed the Real Comedians of Social Media: The Keep Your Distance Comedy Show, which was a great time but not nearly the same as a real-life performance. As a comedian, it was excruciating to not be able to hit stages and rock crowds. I missed hanging out with my peers. As a content creator, however, it may have been one of my most productive years ever, since there wasn't much else to do besides make videos and post to social media.

I did have one memorable opportunity that came my way that year, when I found myself on the radar of the marketing team at the National Park Service. The Park Service is the federal agency tasked with managing the country's national parks, national monuments, and a bunch of other landmarks. This includes well-known vacation sites like Yellowstone and the Grand Canyon, of course, but also memorials such as the Martin Luther King, Jr. Memorial in Washington, D.C., and the Booker T. Washington National Monument in Virginia.

Thing is, while people know a lot of the major sites, there's not always as much activity at some of the lesser-known places. So, in early 2020, the Park Service decided to do a promotional campaign to encourage visitors to spend more time at the other sites. They wanted to make it known that visiting a national park doesn't have to be only about hiking or camping or white water rafting. And, just as important, the message was that taking trips to the national parks wasn't only for white people, that Black families and other people of color were just as welcome and would find as good a time at these places as anyone else. They tapped me to be the spokesperson for the campaign.

It seemed like an ideal fit, given that I'd grown up taking trips with my own family. We didn't have a lot of money when I was young, but that didn't stop my dad from getting us out of the house. He believed that travel was important and family even more important. So while we may have been poor relative to some other families—a kid may have had newer toys than me or a newer bike—my dad always managed to find a way to get our family on the road. Now, mind you, we only traveled to church events in places like Phoenix or Albuquerque. In hindsight, all those cities sucked. Didn't matter then, though. At that time in my life, every outing was a big deal. *Oh my gosh, we're going to eat!*

Now that I'd become a father myself, I was just as adamant about making sure that my sons got a chance to travel—though hopefully to places a little more exciting than a church meeting in New Mexico. Up until then, we'd go hike occasionally, but the only national park I'd visited with my kids was the Martin Luther King, Jr. Memorial in Washington, D.C.

So along comes this National Park Service offer. The meetings were great, always upbeat and positive. Everyone was eager to get something rolling. We kicked around a bunch of ideas, like me doing a comedy show at a national park, but what we settled on was a campaign where I'd be filmed doing stuff with my family like hiking, rafting, and camping. These were things I'd have been doing with my family anyway, but now I'd be getting paid for it. I was down for that.

Then came the catch: Because the Park Service is a government agency and this would be a government contract, they stressed to me that I was not to disparage the government in any way—and, specifically, not the president. As in President Donald Trump. No matter what Trump said, no matter what he did, I wasn't to criticize him in any way. The conversations were really funny, too, because even though we only talked on the phone, I was 97 percent certain that the Park Service representatives I was talking to were Black people. They were like, "Look, man, we know, all right? We work for the government; we know who the president is. *We* can't say stuff, you know what I'm saying? We are aware, and we understand you are going to feel how you feel. But just during the window of this campaign, if you could please not say anything . . . It'll disqualify you from the campaign if you say anything disparaging about the President of the United States."

All I kept wondering was, *How big is that campaign window?*

According to the Park Service team, the campaign was supposed to last less than a year. We'd shoot a video in one place, move on, and film me and my wife and kids doing something new elsewhere. All in all, everything would take place over the course of six months, if I remember right.

I figured I could make it six months. Yes, I'm opinionated. I'm a vocal person when I want to be—especially when it comes to issues that affect Black people and our community—but as they emphasized over and over, the campaign would be only six months long. Plus, we were in the early stages of a major global health crisis. With all the important matters piling up on his desk, Trump couldn't possibly do or say anything so stupid that I'd be unable to hold my tongue, right?

Sigh.

I tried. I really did. But as a comedian, I'm loyal to the joke above almost everything. (The only time I can't always be loyal to the joke is with my wife. If it's going to get me in trouble with her, the joke more than likely has to go. But sometimes even if it is going to cause me some marital issues, I still feel the need to say what I gotta say.)

I can't even remember what the crack was exactly, just that I couldn't resist because Trump kept saying some of the most bogus stuff ever during the pandemic.

I think it was the sound bite about injecting bleach or using UV light inside the body to fight COVID. *Man, what was he talking about?* To make matters worse, people were believing that this was the way to fight a killer virus. I just couldn't resist commenting. But I was doing so much with his comments that it may not even have been a remark on my own thread. I may have reposted somebody else's video, because I also recall Sarah Cooper pointing out the quote where he said, "You're gonna have to use medical doctors." Sarah's response was something like, "What other kind of doctors would you use?" I thought that was really funny.

The moment he came out of his mouth with that foolishness, I remember thinking, *I'm not going to hold back.* Remember, I was doing way more virtual content than before. There was nothing else to do. I was doing videos and virtual podcasts, and anything I found funny, I spoke on it. The jokes were overflowing. No way could I let the UV light/bleach comment slide.

At the same time, we were trying to wrap up the negotiations with the Park Service. I hadn't signed a contract yet, but we'd already been preparing to film a few videos, and when I shared my ideas with the folks at the Park Service, they had been super responsive. They seemed to love what I was planning—and, honestly, I didn't think they were paying me much mind beyond our meeting. *They can't see everything I post anyway. Everything will be fine.* One joke wouldn't matter much.

So I shot the video they wanted, sent it to them . . . and then things went eerily silent. I went from bantering on the phone with the Park Service reps about our campaign plans to being ghosted by them.

Trying to seem hopeful, my wife suggested that maybe their silence was because of the pandemic. I momentarily thought maybe it was because of an issue with the video I'd created. But when I considered it more, I knew what had severed our communication. *They probably have seen one of the videos I made.* The folks had told me in no uncertain terms that I couldn't make any disparaging comments about the president, but I couldn't resist. We had been so close to signing the paperwork, too! But now that deal was dead. Somehow, they'd found me out.

After I got over the disappointment, though, I realized that it was probably for the best. Just like with the NFL, it was about being true to my values. You're nothing without your authenticity—and you're even less without your integrity. If you're silent about something you believe in, especially as a celebrity or a person of high visibility, people will catch on sooner or later. Being anything less than genuine is a surefire way to cause blowback. It wasn't any different than my situation with the NFL, except in the case of the Park Service, I had accepted the offer first before losing it. A $50,000 endorsement deal flopped because of a wisecrack.

But I kept my integrity and that, to me, is worth way more.

"WE'RE JUST CHILDREN": TOURING WITH FAMILY

Years ago, when I first began touring steadily, I decided that it would be a great idea to bring my kids on the road with me when they weren't in school. As a kid, I felt lucky enough to see Orlando and Albuquerque. Now my kids were flying into places like London. I thought they'd be thrilled. Plus, after previous tours, I was starting to feel bad about leaving them behind.

And at first, they were excited. My oldest son's favorite comedian is Tony Baker—not the man who puts food on his table every day, mind you, but that man's co-worker—so he was especially pumped about getting the chance to watch Tony perform live. He even walked out of the green room to stand near the stage as Tony breezed through his brilliant routine. He loved every minute of it. Next was my turn. Before I even walked out, Isaiah had turned around and gone back inside the green room!

Well, at least my younger son was happy to see me.

Not long after we visited London that year, though, I stopped taking the boys out on tour.

And no, it wasn't because my oldest liked Tony more than he liked the man who helped bring him into this world and sacrificed daily to give him a good life. Nope, not at all.

Truth is, I stopped taking them because of the demands of our schedule, especially those early lobby calls we'd get to let us know it was time to check out and head to the airport for yet another leg of the tour. When I say early, I mean bleary-eyed, middle-of-the-night, sleepwalking-in-pajamas early. One time, we were leaving Boston and got a lobby call at three in the morning. My son literally started crying when I woke him up. "We're just children!" he shouted, tears streaming down his face.

And I knew he was right. The boys were on tour because I felt guilty. I loved sharing my success with my sons, but I didn't want to get to the point of *imposing* it on them. As fun as it might've been on certain dates, they deserved better than to be dragged around from one whistle-stop to the next with a bunch of working adults. We got them a babysitter instead. Then, the next year, my son grew sad because he said we travel too much. As a result, my wife decided to stop touring to give them balance.

I still feel bad about leaving them behind as much as I do, but now that they're older, we all handle it a lot better. Plus, they know they can come out whenever they want to catch a show featuring the man who would gladly lay down his life in an instant if it meant securing their futures—or, y'know, Tony Baker.

AWARD MIX-UP

In 2022, I received my second-ever nomination for a major award: the NAACP Image Award for Best Social Media Personality. My first nomination was the year earlier in the same category—but that year I was competing against Tabitha Brown. I tried with all my heart to garner enough votes to win, but c'mon. She's *Tabitha Brown,* the Emmy-winning creator of the *Tab Time* kids' show on YouTube, the vegan TikTok icon, the actress who's appeared everywhere from *The Chi* to *Good Morning America.* Even some of my friends were like, "Kev, I love you—but I REALLY love Tab." I mean, *I* voted for Tab that year.

To be honest, I didn't think I was going to get nominated the year after I lost to Tabitha, but I did. And, once again, I was in the category with a lot of other hot content creators. Nominees included Eunique Jones Gibson, who'd created the powerful "Because of Them We Can" campaign, and Lynae Vanee, the TikTok personality and genius behind the *Parking Lot Pimpin'* series that blended pop culture with political issues. There also was La'Ron Hines, who'd gone viral countless times thanks to his awesome *Are You Smarter Than a Preschooler?* series, and singer/producer Terrell Grice, who had risen to fame via the celebrity interviews he conducted on YouTube.

The competition was stiff, no doubt, but I liked my chances. And I grew even more confident after I showed up at the event and overheard an overexcited production assistant shout into her walkietalkie, "He's here! He's here! Let's start the show. I'll head to the trophy room now!" *Well now,* I thought. *Looks like I'm the winner tonight!*

I lost.

La'Ron Hines took the award instead. Thing was, I was so confident that I was going to win that I was already starting to stand when they called my . . . er, La'Ron's name. As if that wasn't awkward enough, I tried to play it off by walking over to dap him up, but he didn't even see me. Walked on by and gathered up his trophy. *Womp, womp.*

Fortunately, the NAACP was gracious enough to let me come back a third year, when I was nominated in two categories. Melissa and I were up for Outstanding Literary Work—Debut Author for our bestselling book *Marriage Be Hard.* And once again I was up for Outstanding Social Media Personality of the Year. We lost out in the lit category, but I did manage to win the social media award. And this time, I was smart enough to wait until I heard them call *my* name before I got out of my seat. Luckily for me, this time around it was a bigger show than the other two times. In 2021 it was all virtual. In 2022, it was awarded at a party. But in 2023 it was the premier award. We had video packages all throughout the night. Big celebs like Samuel L. Jackson and Angela Bassett were in the room. Shoot, Method Man was sitting at my table! So I guess it worked out in the end.

MY GREATEST LOSS

The worst day of my life started off pleasantly enough.

It was the morning of September 22, 2022, and I was wrapping up a five-mile hike not too far from where we were living in Los Angeles. I had just started exercising regularly in hopes of keeping a promise to myself to be in the best shape of my life by age forty. (Didn't happen.) Earlier that morning, I'd awakened to a text from Jason to a group chat that he and I shared with our good friends Anthony Davis and Ken Telsee.

As I bantered back and forth with Ant and Kenny, I felt my cellphone vibrate. I checked the screen. It was Tami, my brother's wife. I answered the call.

"Hey, Tami, what's up?"

When she spoke, her voice was heavy with a dread like nothing I'd ever heard before. She started talking, quickly and through tears. She proceeded to tell me that Jason had had a seizure while he was driving their son, Julian, to school. My brother was unconscious, she explained. He'd been taken by ambulance to a hospital, where the doctors were working on him.

"I'm on my way there now to be with him," she said before hanging up. "Tell Lis and your dad that I'll call when I have more information."

Click.

Time froze. In my head, I began to detach from my surroundings. You know that camera shot that Spike Lee is famous for, the one where his characters aren't walking but rather look like they're floating aimlessly while the background appears to be receding behind them? That was me, drifting through space/time, trying to make sense of my sister-in-law's words.

I just talked to Jay, I thought.

As Tami's words echoed through the fog that was suddenly clouding my brain, I slowly started to suspect what was happening. *Multiple myeloma.* At first, I tried to shake the idea out of my head. It'd been five years since Jason was diagnosed with the cancer that was leaving holes in his bones. He'd survived a bone marrow transplant. He'd made it back to his family, back to his role as my manager, and back to the life that he lived so passionately. He'd lost weight and several inches in height, but my brother had won that fight.

Sure, the physicians had told us that there wasn't any chance of full remission, but Jay had come as close as I could've imagined. He was so confident in his healing that he would even go around congratulating other people who were in remission from diseases. That's how he was living. My memories flashed back to earlier that same month, when he'd stopped by a book signing that Melissa and I were doing in Houston. We'd gone out to the Four Seasons that evening and had dinner as a family. We'd laughed. We'd drunk. Well, Melissa and I drank. Jay didn't so much as sip liquor.

"I don't know what's wrong with y'all," he'd scolded playfully. "I don't do that type of stuff."

But Jay always had a daring side. Flashing further back, I thought of the summer before, when my wife had planned a family trip to Disneyland. All the kids had come and stayed the night at our house; then we went to the Magic Kingdom and had a blast. Mind you, at Disneyland, many of the rides have signs posted at the entrance that caution you to stay off if you have certain medical conditions. Jason wasn't paying attention to any of that stuff. His whole attitude said, *I'm not going to be afraid. I don't know how much time I have, so I'm living my life to the fullest.*

The fear of losing him had all but faded from memory. As far as I was concerned, he had been healed, and that was supposed to be that.

I'd had a lengthy conversation with him the day before. That day, September 21, Melissa and I had gotten the call that our book *Marriage Be Hard* had landed on the *New York Times* bestseller list. We could hardly believe it. We'd already made the *USA Today* list, so we'd been told there was a chance we'd make the *Times* list, too, but nothing was for certain. Around four o'clock, I was in line waiting to pick up Isaiah from school when my publisher called to let me know we'd earned a spot on the most prestigious bestseller list in the country. Jason, who'd helped us negotiate the book deal, was the first person I texted to tell about the honor. He texted me back right away to congratulate me. He also told me that he was crying tears of happiness.

I celebrated with my wife and her sisters that night and got to bed early. The plan for the next morning was to exercise and then get ready to head out of town for a show I had later that day in San Jose. But the call from Tami had changed all that.

All my sister-in-law told me was that he'd been driving when he'd suddenly gone into convulsions. That was it. I called Melissa to tell her what little I knew. I was still in so much shock that I can't remember exactly what I said or did. I was moving on autopilot, going through the motions without any clear thought. Briefly, I even considered traveling to San Jose as planned and doing my show. Melissa could tell right away that I wasn't thinking right. She was gentle with me.

"I know you want to go to San Jose," she said softly, "but I'm going to go to Houston, just to make sure everything is okay."

She wasn't saying anything directly, but that was her way of letting me know that it'd be best if I canceled the show and went with her to see my brother. I had never before called off a show, not until that moment. But I knew what my wife was driving at.

"I'm going to Houston with you," I agreed.

We went online to buy tickets and could only book seats in the main cabin. For some crazy reason, it hit me right then that I hadn't ridden in coach in a while. Melissa and I were at the point where, if we were trying to go somewhere and couldn't find first-class seats, we probably weren't going to go, not if we could help it. This time around, I could care less. My bougie pretensions dried up quickly. We reserved a pair of uncomfortable seats in row 38 of a United Airlines flight to Houston, and we continued to wait to hear back from Tami.

I texted back and forth with Jason's wife and son while we got ready to catch our flight.

"We're in the hospital," came one text from Tami.

"They just took Dad back in an emergency room," my nephew Julian wrote a little later.

Then Julian called me just as we boarded the plane: "Dad's stable. Things look good."

I felt a twinge of relief. Jason was going to be okay. Allowing myself a sliver of hope, I pictured me pulling up on Jason when I arrived in Texas and giving him a piece of my mind. *You cost me money, nigga! Got me missing this show in San Jose because I'm over here freaking out.* I was ready to get down there, hug my brother, and laugh. We boarded the plane and settled in for the three-and-a-half-hour flight from LA.

About an hour into the flight, my phone rang again. It was Julian again. To this day, I have no idea how my phone worked with us thirty-five thousand feet in the air, but it did. He didn't call me on FaceTime audio either. He called me on my cell like a normal phone call. When I answered, I could hear my nephew sobbing.

"Kev . . ." he stammered. "Kev, he's gone."

"What?!" I shouted into the phone. "What do you mean *gone?*"

"He . . . he's gone. Something went wrong. He's gone."

Just like that, on the afternoon of September 22, 2022, my brother was no longer here.

The official cause was a heart attack. We learned later that Jason's coronary had been brought on by his years-long battle with cancer. The toll the disease had taken was heavier than we'd imagined, and the strain on his body had ultimately become too much.

For a while, it felt like my faith had passed with my brother. People say trust God. But I didn't. People say God don't make mistakes. But it felt like he'd made one this time—or, worse, that he didn't care. I remember thinking about how my brother died even though I'd prayed. My family prayed. His friends prayed. Where was our miracle? He made a shirt that said, *I Have a Powerful Testimony,* but now he was dead. Where's the testimony in that? I didn't understand then and I don't understand now. I just sit with the truth that sometimes bad stuff happens. There's no ultimate great plan. No lesson that we need to learn. Sometimes bad stuff happens, and that's it. It just sucks, and you have to figure out how to keep living.

It's been a few years since he's passed, but the hole in my heart, not to mention my life, still hasn't closed. And it most certainly can never be filled by anything else. Jay was my greatest friend, one of my biggest influences and most ardent supporters. Believe it or not, I fired him officially as my manager in 2021—at least technically— because he admitted that he wasn't interested in helping me pursue any more endorsement deals. Talking about, "I'm not an outbound call guy."

He was being honest, though. Jay didn't have any real Hollywood connections, not the ones I was going to need now that my career had taken off. So I'd had to find new management. But I still kept my brother on payroll. His fee went down some, but he and I never stopped working together.

How could we? Perhaps more than anyone else, my brother helped me become the comedian I am today. He'd come on as my booking manager in 2015, taking over for my homegirl Cherise, who is still one of my good friends but was never built to be a booking manager. She had a full-time job and was so swamped with other responsibilities that she didn't even have time to answer emails consistently. So I had to let her go. (Her mom was mad at me for three years about that!)

But I knew I needed somebody to represent me. I'm a terrible negotiator. I mean, just ask AwesomenessTV. Before Jason stepped in, I was going out and doing stand-up shows for $500. After we agreed that he'd manage me, he stopped accepting $500 as my fee.

"You are worth more than $500," he used to tell me. "And for us to get you above that, we're going to have to start saying 'no' to $500 so that we're able to get you to $1,000. And to get you to $1,500, we're going to have to say 'no' to $1,000."

Soon as he said that, I knew that he cared, because whenever Jason had to tell a potential promoter "no," that meant he wasn't getting paid either. He always wanted only the best deal for me. He would never put me in a position to take less than what I was worth. He's why I landed many of the bookings and earned many of the fees I did. He ran the point on the negotiations for some of my earliest endorsement deals, like my Spectrum TV arrangement. He made sure promoters met my needs on the road, that I had decent places to stay when out of town, that I got proper billing on marquees.

In military families, your familial relationships are often deeper than other people's. You move so much that you don't develop life-long friends the way most people do. Most of the time, you've got each other, and that's about it. But I also loved Jay not just because of our shared background or genetic ties, but because he was a fantastic person. He was a man who'd be my friend if he weren't my brother. Knowing this only deepened the sense of loss.

One of the few things that makes his death easier for me to cope with is that I don't harbor any regrets when it comes to my relationship with my brother. Our love was genuine, our respect mutual. We argued as siblings do, but we only really fell out once. It happened back when we were in our college years and living in Washington. As crazy as it sounds, it's all true. My brother had this "situation" where his girlfriend at the time was secretly living in our parents' house. Yes, you read that right. *Our parents' house!* The home of this super conservative, Pentecostal couple who didn't believe women had any business wearing pants, let alone spending long nights sleeping next to their unmarried son.

But this is how dumb my brother must've thought my dad was. Jason had a back door to his room, right? So each day, his girlfriend, who was a really pretty girl, would hang out at our house for hours at a time, eating, watching TV, just chilling. Then, after it got late, she'd get up and be like, "All right, see you guys later." She'd walk out the front door, and she'd essentially just walk around to the back door and slip into his room. Then they'd just be quiet. When the next morning would come, she would fake "show up" at our house. She'd just walk out the back door of his room, come to the front door and be like, "Hey, good morning, guys. Is Jason here?"

I used to think, *Bro, come on. Everybody knows what's happening!* I think my dad knew but didn't want to believe it. Either that, or he felt like he needed real proof. If the latter was the case, then it wasn't long before he stumbled across just the smoking gun he needed.

One day, I'm in the laundry room with my dad, ironing my

clothes to get ready for school. He's looming over the washer and dryer fishing clothes out of the laundry. Suddenly, my dad pulls this lacy thong out of the washing machine. As you might expect, the man had questions.

"Whose is this?"

I just shrugged my shoulders and said nothing. I ain't no snitch . . .

. . . but we all knew my mom don't wear *those* type of underwear.

When he got in trouble, my brother got mad at me. He believed I snitched on him, even though I told him I didn't. We beefed for probably four months. I was in college, and he was working, so we didn't see each other that much even if we wanted to resolve matters. It was the only time in our lives when my brother and I didn't talk to each other.

Then came Christmas. That holiday, he handed me a card and was like, "I know we ain't talking right now, but you're always my brother." That was really all it took. I loved Jay and had never wanted to be mad with him in the first place. After that, we were the best of friends forever again.

I once saw a tweet from Lupita Nyong'o about Chadwick Boseman's death that kind of summed up my feelings losing my brother. It read, "Grief is the price of love." There's no regret there. There's just a great missing of somebody that you love. What was it that Vision said in *WandaVision*? "What is grief, if not love persevering?"

When you love someone deeply and as passionately as I love my brother, you're going to miss everything about that person when they're gone. I miss being able to text him. I miss knowing how he would be at family events. I miss sharing crazy stories and stupid memes and having pointless sports debates. I miss celebrating even the smallest victories with him.

Even worse than not celebrating with him, I now have to cope with the sad reality that whatever wins I do enjoy will never match what, so far, has been the greatest loss in my life.

WHY I BLAME NIA LONG FOR MY BROTHER'S HEART ATTACK

All right, so I admit right off that the title of this chapter is a little clickbait-y. Nia Long didn't have anything to do with my brother having a heart attack. Actually, the title relates to the punchline of a story I began telling on stage after my brother passed, a story that had unfolded right before I got the horrible news about Jason. Let me explain.

As I said, Jason died on September 22, 2022. Before that, we talked every day. I'd be texting him relentlessly, either directly to his phone or through the group chat that we shared with our friends Ant and Kenny.

Our group chat was sacred, mind you. I contend that in this day and age, everybody needs that group chat where they can share the funniest things and make their darkest jokes. It's a place for you to vent, where you can spitball outside-the-box ideas with people you know and trust before sharing them with strangers. The chat can help you sharpen ideas or convince you to discard them altogether.

Best of all, it helps prevent you from posting dumb stuff online. As they say: *Keep that in the group chat!*

That September morning, the group had gotten a text from my brother. I was exercising so I had to jump into the chat a little late. As it turned out, my brother had shared a video clip from the comedian and impressionist Savvy Amusing, who's known for dubbing completely fabricated conversations over videos of actual celebrities talking. In Jay's clip, Savvy Amusing had overdubbed former Boston Celtics head coach Ime Udoka's speech at a press conference. In the dub, Savvy Amusing had Ime explaining why he had cheated on the gorgeous Nia Long, then his wife, with some random woman in the Celtics organization. The video had our entire group chat cracking up. I replied with a "ha ha!" in the chat. Kenny texted emojis and asked, "Bro, they trying to suspend Ime the whole season?!!"

I responded that I'd noticed the impending season-long punishment, too, and explained that "I think it's cuz she's on staff. If it was a regular person not affiliated probably nothing happens to him."

The conversation eventually switched to the woman people thought Ime cheated with. Kenny posted a picture of her in the chat and said, "She looks better than Nia to me."

Then he said the unthinkable: "I think my gf looks better than Nia Long."

"Nigga," I responded, "Nia Long looks better than your girl."

"Why because she's famous?!" he texted back.

"Because she's Nia Long!"

"I'll put my girl up against any celebrity!"

As you might gather, Kenny loves hard—clearly to the point of delusion. He wasn't just spouting off either. Kenny really believed that when he said it. And that's why, as his dearest friends, we had to stop him in his tracks.

Ant and I spent the next few minutes trying to bring Kenny back to reality. We reminded him that, celebrity or not, Nia Long was one of the finest actresses around. Kenny's girlfriend was not ugly, of course. But Nia Long? Nia Long was world-class fine. Hall of Fame fine. But no matter how much we insisted, Kenny wasn't buying it. His girl was prettier, he kept insisting. All of us were having a great laugh.

Then, as the three of us were joking and jabbing at each other on text, I got the phone call that changed my life.

At that point, I said onstage, I scrolled back through the chat and realized my brother hadn't posted anything after Kenny claimed his girlfriend was without a doubt finer than Nia Long.

"I think that text is what did it!" I exclaim.

That was the punchline I used when I next hit the stage after Jay's funeral. My brother had seen Kenny's outlandish contention and thought, *Welp, that's it for me!*

The line got hearty laughs. More important, it helped me heal. Jay would have thought it was hilarious. When I see him again, I'm gonna ask him to confirm that that's really what happened.

HOW I BECAME AN ACOLYTE
OF THE ILLUMINATI

U sed to be a time when I couldn't wait to be accused of being in
the Illuminati.

To my mind, back in the day, I would know that I'd made it big
in comedy when some internet conspiracy theorist finally took to
The Shade Room or YouTube to start a rumor that KevOnStage had
secretly joined the infamous, blood-soaked, super-secret society hell-
bent on global domination. I mean, take a trip to just about any
Black community in America, and you're gonna find any number of
people with a mile-long list of all the Black celebrities they firmly
believe achieved fame and fortune by joining the Illuminati or par-
taking in one of its many Satanic rituals. You're nobody, it seems,
until somebody accuses you of joining in blood sacrifices and pagan
orgies with record executives and political leaders and movie studio
chiefs.

You're a rapper with a string of hit records? A comedian with several Netflix specials to her name? An actor who just won an Oscar?

With a lot of Black folks, it can be explained one of two ways: Either the superstar in question has had someone killed by the Illuminati, or (if he's a man) he's getting paid off for wearing a dress in a movie or TV show—and thus furthering what conspiracy theorists insist is a gay agenda promoted by the Illuminati. Can you imagine that? The Illuminati taking a break from its schemes to rule the world to do diversity outreach? The DEI-lluminati. But the illogic of that doesn't matter to some. However you slice it, to them, the Illuminati is always behind it all.

Now, you'd think something like this, if true, might cause alarm and have folks speaking in panicked whispers. But nope. Black people tell stories like this all the time, at restaurants, on street corners, and, of course, most frequently in the most trusted source of all the crazy conspiracies circulating through Black America—the barbershop.

I can remember being a kid and staring, almost as if hypnotized, as the older men sat around the shop weaving one nutty conspiracy theory into another, shaping their crazy stories all while the barbers sculpted bald fades and Afros. *The Protocols of the Elders of Zion. Behold a Pale Horse.* The Willie Lynch letter. And most terrifying of all, the Illuminati.

Was it crazy talk? Sure. But was it entertaining? Without a doubt. Also, as ludicrous as the conclusions are, the reason ideas like this take hold in communities like where I grew up is because Black people know what it's like to be conspired against in real life. By actual powerful forces. We've seen whole communities slaughtered, towns burned to the ground, good men and women killed, all because Black people had the audacity to try to aspire to more than what some others felt they deserved. Given the extraordinary lengths society sometimes has gone to to ensure Black failure, why wouldn't some of us then be inclined to explain Black successes in equally outrageous and extraordinary terms?

On the other hand, some niggas just want to be fake "deep."

In either case, alleged membership in the Illuminati has become something of a measuring stick for the accomplishments of successful Black entertainers, politicians, athletes, and businesspeople. Membership changes from weekend to weekend, city to city, and depending on who's sitting in the barber's chair that day. Sometimes, Jay-Z is in the Illuminati, along with Beyoncé. Denzel Washington is a standing member, as are Spike Lee, Lil Nas X, and Barack Obama. Like I said, if Black people aren't accusing you of being in or working for the Illuminati, you haven't achieved a certain level of fame yet.

As for me, I always assumed the conspiracy brothers would get at me on the dress front. That's because, back when we used to do Playmakers, me, my brother Jason, and our friend Ant had come up with a video skit called "Stuff Black Church Girls Say" that we wrote for our wives. A simple parody of the everyday conversations we heard from Black women, it seemed like a hilarious idea to us. But our wives disagreed. They didn't find it compelling at all. And they all refused to do it.

So, as guys who grew up bingeing Martin Lawrence, we were like, "Well, nigga, we'll play the characters!" And we did, occasionally donning wigs and blouses to mock some of the funnier things we would overhear from women in church. I didn't care then about the criticism, and I don't care now. Like Martin, we were part of a time-honored tradition of Black men dressing up in the name of humor, nothing more. It was no different than *Big Momma's House* or Tyler Perry's Madea character or Jamie Foxx's Wanda.

This was well before I'd seen any measure of success, mind you. Back then, I figured that by the time people were making crazy allegations like that, that would mean that I'd struck gold in my career, that I was wildly rich and enviably famous. It would mean I was on billboards that line Hollywood Boulevard and Times Square. (I've been on billboards before, but I mean billboards everywhere!) It would mean that I moved around in helicopters and limos, aboard yachts and private planes. It would mean I owned apartment buildings, entire city blocks, maybe even an island.

So when the conspiracists really did come for me, in 2024, I was partly surprised, because I hadn't achieved even a fraction of what some of my more successful entertainment peers had. I also was angered, because the allegations aimed at me were a heartbreaking illustration of cruelty and stupidity.

Basically, what it came down to was that some idiots had decided to post on social media that I had "sacrificed" my brother, the same brother whose death has left me heartbroken to this day, just so that I could rub elbows with a few Hollywood celebs. The rumor started after I posted a few pictures I'd taken with Kevin Hart at a function for his Hartbeat entertainment company and, earlier, with Will Smith and Martin Lawrence as part of a promotional campaign I'd been tapped to do on behalf of the release of *Bad Boys: Ride or Die.*

I was getting comments like, "I always knew he was Illuminati. Now look, proof." "Only way to explain how he is meeting these people is Illuminati."

In Kevin Hart's case, I'd met him twice before we took our photo, once at a Hartbeat brunch a couple of years ago and another time at a birthday party at his studio. During the first two meetings, I only was able to exchange the Black man "head nod" with him and dap him up. Otherwise, I stayed out of his way. But at the next Hartbeat brunch, we ended up having a full conversation.

Melissa and I had arrived early to the party—we were already tired when we got there because we're old—and we found someplace to sit down. We're all the way on the opposite side of the party, at the other end of the house, having some lamb chops and a drink. I was talking to a DJ friend of ours, but otherwise it's relatively quiet and there's nobody else around.

We're chopping it up, about to eat some lamb chops, when all of a sudden we hear this commotion. We look up, and Kevin Hart's walking in with his team all around him. Loud whispers followed his footsteps. *Oh, Kevin Hart. There's Kevin Hart.*

Honestly, I was excited to see him, too, but we're, y'know, professional peers. So I'm telling myself, *Okay, be cool. Be cool. Let's just be cool. Everybody be cool.*

He talks to a few people. They take a few pictures, then he comes to me and is like, "Yo, Kev, what's up? I see everything you're doing, and I'm a fan. I see how you move. I see the business mindset you have." And he was sincere, too. He talked about my work on social media. He mentioned a tour I had just kicked off with Tony Baker that we'd dubbed the Bald Brothers tour.

"I want you to come through the office and meet the team," he said.

I'd already been to the office and met *a* team at Hartbeat. I've done three brand deals with them. But this time, he meant *his* team. He stands there, and Kevin Hart pours into me for a full seven or eight minutes. Everybody is standing around waiting to talk to this man, but he does not rush. He makes sure he gets every word he wants to say to me out and I take it all in. Then he takes a few pictures with me. (I'm sure I was the one who asked for them.) Melissa and I left that party so high on the hog!

Mind you, my interaction with Kevin Hart had come on the back end of what would wind up as probably my best week ever as a professional entertainer. Earlier that same week, Sony Pictures had me working with Will Smith and Martin Lawrence on a project related to the rollout of their fourth *Bad Boys* movie. Initially, I was just working with them on a sketch that would be used to tease the film. As is the case with projects like that, I ended up having to edit that thing and turn it in eighteen different times. In one version, the music was too loud. Another version needed to be cut to two minutes. Another version needed a different type of camera shot. Then I had to return a clip that I had originally been asked to trim. I had to get approval from Will's team. I also needed Martin's team to approve. Then the studio had to like it. I'd turn in that version and then nobody liked it. I edited that thing every day for a week and a half, bringing in new versions two or three times a day.

Meanwhile, even as I'm getting the clip together, an executive from the agency handling the rollout approached me with an unexpected offer. "We're going to be doing a screening this week. And we were curious: Would you mind hosting it?"

In my head I'm like, *Are you crazy? I get to introduce Will Smith and Martin Lawrence? Oh God! Yes!*

Mind you, at first I thought they were talking about me hosting the premiere, which really would've been crazy. Actually, they just meant a fan screening that they'd set up. It didn't really matter. The opportunity still meant the world to me.

Before the screening started, I was able to go with my family backstage to talk over the intro with Will and Martin. Will sees me, and he's like, "Oh, Kev. Hey, man. This is a lot of work, but it's always better when you're around." I was hyped. Even better, my kids got a chance to see it, too. (Take that, Tony Baker!) At that point, I had become Cool Dad, which is very hard to come by with teenage boys nowadays.

The fan screening went great, too. Martin and Will came out, tossed candy to the crowd, and even took the time to mug with me for selfies on the stage. When Sony asked me to post the images on social media, I didn't hesitate. Photos with Kevin Hart, Will Smith, and Martin Lawrence all in one week? I had to be living right, I thought.

Overwhelmingly, the responses were positive. We're talking like 99.9999998 percent of them happy, upbeat, and congratulatory. But there were also a handful of crazy allegations. The same sort of weird conspiracy theorists who constantly smeared Will and his family, who accused Martin of carrying forward some perverse agenda because he dressed as a woman in *Big Momma's House,* were now at my social media gates. One tweet in particular stoked my ire the most.

"Man, you can tell," the poster wrote, "that he sacrificed his brother to get to this moment."

Instantly, all the joy I'd relished in that week seemed to dry up. I couldn't believe someone actually took the time to put that on my timeline. It was just some random dude I don't know, but the remark still stung. I deleted the comment and blocked him. *You're never going to be able to comment on my posts again.* But I'd already seen his. I don't know if I could have felt more misunderstood in that moment.

I get that to some people I'm a celebrity. I've got millions of followers. I make great money. I get the privilege of working with some of the most talented people in the digital world. But I still couldn't help wondering why people looking in would think life happens any differently for me than it does for them—at least in the ways that truly matter. I have friends who've lost their siblings around my age. One of my close friends from El Paso lost two of her siblings and she hadn't even turned forty. But because she works a traditional nine-to-five job, nobody's going to ever say she sacrificed her siblings for a promotion.

You think I'd trade my brother's life for a picture with Kevin Hart or a chance to work with Will Smith? Nigga, we grew up poor! The worst job I've ever worked was a short-lived gig I had doing lawn care for the City of Tacoma, where I picked up trash and cigarette butts outside a courthouse all day. A close second was when I used to spend all day grilling onions for this burger joint. I'd come home every day smelling like a bucketload of Walla Walla onions.

Trust me, I would *gladly* do either one of those jobs until I'm ninety-five years old if Jason could come back. I would have nothing. I would walk the streets foraging for food if it meant he got to live more. I don't care about this stuff more than I care about my blood brother.

So yeah, I blocked and deleted the guy, but the damage was already done.

For a long time, I wondered how people could be so callous and so dumb. I mean, in all seriousness, my career is almost singularly tied to the internet. There is not only proof of how I clawed my way up, there is a digital roadmap of my success. You can go back on my YouTube page and trace every success that I've had. Every big viral video, every significant career moment, every project that's coming out, there's proof of all that online.

Furthermore, that Illuminati nonsense diminishes the work we do, the efforts we put forth. It assumes that Hollywood has picked you out of everybody, invited you to the secret room where everybody's wearing masks and blood, and said, "Hey, you sell your soul to us now, and then we will pick you out and make you the greatest." And then flames fan out, there's a devil's shadow in the background, and suddenly you have a hundred million dollars. I'm supposed to be like *Oh, nooo, my soul . . .*

But the truth is much easier to grasp. Nobody's taking those kinds of shortcuts. I just worked really hard for a long time, and eventually things started working out. I haven't hosted *Saturday Night Live*. I haven't had a big movie on Netflix. I have a Spectrum TV commercial that's been running for four or five years. I sold a show to BET. These are still possible without the Illuminati's help.

Besides, I'm a church kid still doing a lot of church-related humor. You know how the Illuminati works. You got to serve the devil, man. You got to give it up for big Lucifer. I would imagine if I was Illuminati, I wouldn't be able to talk about God anymore. I'd be under Hollywood control.

In the end, those kinds of mean-spirited rumors illustrate one of the worst parts of being a celebrity—the high visibility placed on so much of your life. When other people lose family, they get to grieve in a different way. When you're a public figure, people feel entitled to your business. People are nosy in general, so when someone dies in anybody's life, people want to know what happened. But when you have four or five million fans, not only do you get that, you get much more speculation. People talk about it on podcasts. People put fake YouTube videos up saying they know how your family died. You're asked to grieve and deal with the public at the same time. You're expected to talk about your grief to the press and on podcasts. It's the worst way to have to deal with the worst things that can happen in your life.

Sometimes, success can be an even bigger drag than failure.

ATTENDING A SEX SHOW
IN AMSTERDAM

When I travel to a city, I like to experience what that place is best known for. Food, architecture, museums—whatever the thing to do is in that city, I try to do it. One year, I was overseas with Tahir Moore and Tony Baker as part of the Real Comedians of Social Media Tour, and we found ourselves with a ten-day break between performances in the UK. While we were waiting, I decided to take the team on vacation. We agreed to go to the Netherlands for three days, Spain for another four, and then head back to England to wrap up our shows in Birmingham and London.

True to my travel habits, when we hit Amsterdam, I made sure my friends and I dove into as much of the local scene as possible. We visited the Anne Frank House. We ate herring, stroopwafels, and poffertjes. We didn't buy any drugs, which, along with prostitution, are famously legal in Amsterdam—but I still will never forget the sight of seeing a pack of ecstasy available in that city's equivalent of a 7-Eleven. I also won't forget all the adults who weren't hosting kids' birthday parties but were nonetheless hawking a curiously large number of balloons. I thought it odd, tweeted about it, and soon learned that those balloons contained laughing gas that was for sale. So no, none of the legal drugs that Amsterdam is known for.

As for the prostitution . . .

We went through the city's red-light district and, sho' nuff, they claimed to be selling sex. While wandering around, I picked up a flyer for a live sex show. *No way*, I thought. *That can't be real. I mean, I get it, it's Amsterdam. But . . . no way.*

Despite my doubts, the crew and I decided to check it out. Whatever this show *really* was, I assumed that we would get tricked, enjoy a good laugh, and have a funny story to tell friends. The only thing the skeptic in me kept wondering was, *How they gonna fake sex?*

We arrived at the theater at midnight, minutes before the show was set to begin. Not long after we take our seats did two people come out from behind the curtain. Dude's peen was already fully hard. They lay down on what basically amounted to a huge, spinning lazy Susan. He lubes his meat up and goes to pound town.

Ahem . . . Well then. Guess it really was a live sex show. My bad for doubting you, Amsterdam. I'll *never* make that mistake again.

THAT TIME I PISSED OFF A
FAMOUS CELEBRITY

Let's get this out of the way off top: No, I will not reveal the celebrity's name because, frankly, I don't want no more smoke.

Suffice it to say that I have a hard time understanding how far and wide my videos go, and one time this famous actor (who I'll only say appeared in a multibillion-dollar movie franchise) was pissed at me. He did something funny, and I, like all of America, decided to make fun of it. As I do with most of my videos, I checked the engagement numbers for the day and moved on. The video wasn't doing that well, hadn't gone viral. As far as I was concerned, it was a dud, so I moved on.

Because of this, I was more than a little shocked one day when a comedian I knew hit me and was like, "Yo! That even more famous actor from the multibillion-dollar movie franchise is mad at you."

Me?! For what?!

"He wants you to check your DMs," the comedian told me.

Another surprise. I don't have my DMs open to anyone I don't follow. Too many notifications. I checked my DMs, and, sho' nuff, there were his messages, staring back at me from my phone. One series read:

Bro . . . We cool right?

Delete the post . . . Respectfully we ain't never had no problems on any level.

Respectfully delete the post thank you.

Another: *Yo . . . sent you a dm thanks*

So I responded: *You got it. No harm meant.*

Mega-famous person: *Thank you.*

Me: *You're welcome.*

I won't name the movie franchise. I don't want people trying to figure out who it is. Every time I've said something about this person, no matter how many people on the internet are talking about him, he always finds *me*. There's no problem between us, mind you. And I'm not afraid of the brother. I just don't want no smoke. And believe me, when he decides to trip, he be trippin'!

The crazy thing is, he's one of the nicest people ever. I'd met him in person long before I made my joke. I didn't think he knew who I was, but he was super nice. Still, he did not take kindly to my joke.

To tell you the truth, I never even thought he'd pay attention. If you're traditionally famous—which I've never seen myself as being—I picture you as being on set all day. You're too busy for Instagram. But what I found about the stars is, those folks are no different than you and me. They're on Instagram, TikTok, just like anybody else, knowing more than I think they'd be knowing. Way more. You may not think they pay attention. Heck, they may want you to *think* they're not paying attention. But take it from your boy, they are.

My wife says my problem is that I underestimate how many people know me. It didn't happen every time—still, more times than I can count, when everyone seemed to make a video commenting on something, I would be the only one to get a DM asking for mine to be removed.

Melissa warned me that I had to stop making videos about celebrities because one was gon' pull up on me one day. True to form, I ain't listen then. I'm listening now.

RAZOR FACE

Years ago, a well-known multinational grooming company approached me trying to get its hands on what then passed for my beard.

The corporation had just developed a new electric razor that it insisted was designed specifically to prevent a man's face from breaking out in bumps after a shave. For a lot of men, and for Black men especially, razor bumps can pose a seriously uncomfortable obstacle when it comes to grooming. Our skin tends to be coarser, so we run a greater risk of shaved hair becoming ingrown, growing back into the skin and thus causing razor bumps. In the past few years, full beards have become the trendy grooming statement among Black men, but I'd always been unwilling to put up with the skin irritation that comes from grooming them. In fact, just before this company reached out to me, I'd done a lengthy video detailing some of our grooming woes and explaining how desperately I wanted a shave that was clean and comfortable. Since the company's marketing team was targeting its new razor to brothers and knew that I often talked about my shaving issues, they decided I'd be an ideal spokesman for their "revolutionary" new shaver.

I was excited when they got in touch. I knew what it felt like to enjoy a shave only to have your chin develop the texture of a Seagram's gin bottle a day later. The company swore up and down that this time would be different. It also didn't hurt that they were offering a considerable amount of money—high five figures for a single video—to take their razor for a test drive. All I had to do was shoot a video of me shaving on camera and tell everybody how awesome the razor was.

Everything about this endorsement seemed perfectly aligned: a product I needed and would use, a reputable company, a fee worth more than what I could earn in an entire year at KeyBank. Easy. I mean, it wasn't like I was being asked to keep quiet while a crazy politician let a killer virus ravage the country, right?

So not long after we struck the deal, the shaver arrives. Following the operating instructions carefully, I put it through its paces on video, carefully showcasing how the hot new "anti-bumping" technology in the razor blade was made especially for men who frequently suffer from ingrown hairs. When I was done, my face felt great! My chin, cheeks, and neck were as smooth as they'd ever been. Thrilled at the idea that this thing actually worked, I edited the video quickly and immediately turned it over to the grooming company.

When I shoot an endorsement video, it usually takes four or five days for the company or its ad/marketing agency to get back to me with editorial notes, which I then use as guidelines for editing the new version of the video. However, before the company could get back to me, my face had started to feel strange. By the second day after I'd shaved, my chin and cheeks were tingling. By the third day, my face had broken out in full-blown irritation.

"No!" I shouted, turning my face left to right in the bathroom mirror, ingrown hairs raising more bumps with each passing hour. "No, no, no, noooo!"

It kept getting worse.

By the fourth day, I still hadn't gotten notes back, but my skin was so messed up that I was reaching out to the razor manufacturer's marketing team instead of waiting for them to call me.

"Hey, man," I told them. "I'm sorry, but my face is all bumped up. I know one of the claims in the videos is that you won't bump up, but that's just not the case. I don't know what y'all want me to do."

It was a depressing admission to have to make. First off, I really was excited about the razor and its potential to provide Black men with relief from razor bumps. Also, I was looking forward to being a spokesperson on other products for such a huge brand, as they paid great. I didn't want to miss out on the bag and have my own face all messed up, to boot.

Not long after that, I got a note back from the brand or its ad agency—I can't remember exactly which. They said, "Hey, if you don't mind, we don't mind, because your face doesn't have any bumps in the video. Technically you're not lying. So if you don't mind posting it, we will still pay you for it."

The offer was certainly tempting. To their point, the video showed a successful shave. My face was flawless. If it broke out two days after the fact, could I really blame the razor? How could I say with certainty that there wasn't some other factor that had caused the bumping? It wasn't like the grooming company was gonna tell on me.

But then I thought about my followers, about all the people from all sorts of backgrounds who put some measure of trust in the things I say. Then I started picturing all those men who would try this razor because I told them about it but would still find themselves grappling with skin problems. *If I take this money, somebody, even if it's just one person, is going to be like, "Oh snap, I've been afraid of shaving my head because of fear of razor bumps. But I trust Kev . . ."*

I pictured all the angry guys, faces looking like Killmonger's chest, emailing me and posting on my social media pages, like, "Not you, Kev! Did you know?"

I didn't feel good about it at all. I couldn't sleep at night knowing full well that I was lying in that video. So I broke the news to the marketers: "Man, this ain't right. I can't post it. And I can't accept the money."

Now, here's God's blessing to me. After that razor fiasco, my wife told me I'd need to let my beard grow out so I could get my skin together. My brother Jay, who used to be a barber, told me that same thing. The whole time, though, I'm under the impression that I couldn't grow a full beard, or that, if I did, it'd turn out hideous. But I decided to take Melissa's advice and let it grow—and let her help me with it. Ever supportive, she would stay up with me and pick every single ingrown hair on my face with tweezers. Each time I got a bump, she worked on that bad boy by hand. Next thing I know, probably like six weeks later, I had a little beard! *Oh snap!* It would take years for it to fill in, but eventually, it came in thick and robust, all salt-and-peppery. These days, my beard game is rock solid. I'm talking about the full-on, lustrous, Black Thought, Afro Santa, chin-stroking wise man joint. I love it!

But I never would've had it if it weren't for that brand deal gone wrong. I would've cut it, convinced that I couldn't grow it. I still have some razor bumps under my chin, which will probably never go away. But they aren't standing up all over my face anymore. And my skin is a thousand times clearer and cleaner than it used to be.

Not long after Razorgate, I wound up landing an endorsement deal with another grooming product maker, a company called Bevel. Their razors actually work on me. I never get razor bumps using Bevel products. On top of that, they're great partners who've worked with me countless times. They don't even have to pay me for all I do. Sometimes I make content featuring their products because it just makes sense to what I'm doing. And I just like them, so I don't mind throwing some love their way.

As for the company that I tried to do that first endorsement deal with, they're still around. They're probably too big to fail anyway. And that razor they wanted me to promote? It's still on the market. They've recruited some other brand ambassadors who have been more than happy to try to sell people on that same razor. And, hey, maybe their faces aren't bumping up three days after their videos. I can't say.

I'm certainly not accusing them of being out here lying for a check. I just know that neither fans nor my face would ever forgive me if I did.

AN APP FOR THAT

If the first ten or fifteen years of my career were marked by constant failures, the early 2020s, the years since I struck out on my own with the Real Comedians of Social Media Tour in 2019, have been defined by rousing successes.

All the hard work I'd put in over those early years was at last paying dividends. The content that I was churning out kept getting better, funnier, sharper. And it was turning me into a ubiquitous figure across social media. From Facebook to Twitter to YouTube, millions were tuning in to watch the skits, sketches, and short video commentaries I posted each day. Additionally, I was touring the country and performing overseas with other top-notch digital-age comedians. Strong working relationships with ad agencies and with some of the largest brands in the country were allowing me to do lucrative promotional work for everyone from Spectrum TV to Sony Pictures. I rubbed shoulders with some of the most colossal names in entertainment, and Melissa and I, still very much in love, became bestselling authors together. My sons and my nephew were healthy and growing. And, although I still ached for my late brother Jason, the rest of my family was doing fine. My parents and sister were hanging in there. Not to mention, my bank account was coming along quite nicely, too.

The Fredericks Family Manifest Destiny Plan (yes, I know, the name still sucks) was running in overdrive.

But of course, for all my achievements, it never felt like enough. Success will do you that way. You get a taste, and you want more. You get more, and you start looking around for new spaces to conquer. As long as you make sure to appreciate what you already have, there's nothing wrong with extending your reach even further. Accomplishment isn't just its own reward, it's also a motivational force.

In 2020, I found myself lingering over the one ambition I'd never fulfilled. I wanted to do a feature project. I'd tried my hand at writing a few TV and movie scripts, but nothing had ever come of them. Other than my brief turn alongside my son in *The Little Rascals Save the Day*, I'd made little impact on big-screen productions and even less in television. I had writing credits thanks to the skits I'd created for my sons and myself, but that wasn't the same as seeing a script turned into a full-length production. Whenever I'd gone to any of the industry bigwigs like Russell Simmons or Brian Robbins about my film and TV ideas, they'd politely rebuffed me. Maybe the ideas weren't my best, but just like I knew that I could succeed in stand-up and that I could make it in LA as an entertainer, I wanted to prove that I could do more than crank out digital posts, funny shorts, and observational jokes.

My brother was the first one to make me realize that if I wanted to do that, I'd have to be more than just a screenwriter.

"Instead of waiting for someone else to put your content out, why not do it yourself?" he asked, almost casually, one day. "Why not create your own streaming service to distribute your material?"

It was a masterstroke. I'd already learned the hard way that I'd be waiting forever if I kept going to movie executives to pick up my ideas. Meanwhile, 2020 had already been pretty much canceled by the pandemic. Wasn't nothing going on. So me and my friends got to work building out a new home where all my content, past, present, and future, would live. Tony Baker introduced us to Transit Pictures, a video production company that could help us get original programming off the ground. Melissa and I, as well as friends like Tony, Tahir Moore, and Angel Moore (aka That Chick Angel), took our own money and began investing in an app that would host the content. Lis and I took what we'd earned from the paid Patreon page I had launched in 2018 and, along with the others, supplemented it with money we'd made from the earlier tours as well as the pandemic-ready, virtual-only tour we'd launched earlier that year.

The video company Vimeo came on board as a partner, offering to provide viewers access to our video content. None of this was cheap, of course. It wasn't easy to do either. But after months of toiling and testing, we finally settled on a program that we were happy with. Before the year was out, the KevOnStage Studios app rolled out to the Apple and Google Play stores.

In the beginning, the app, which cost a mere $6 monthly to access, teemed with content. A lot of the digital material that I was sharing across other channels, such as my Patreon material, soon migrated over to the app. Angel, Tony, and Tahir brought their own brands of genius as well.

And for a while, it went great. Or at least, we thought it did. When we first launched, we got something like forty-one thousand subscribers in a matter of weeks, at $5.99 a pop. I was thinking, *Oh my God, this is going to be super lucrative!* Forty-one thousand times six came to $246,000 a month. To my mind, a quarter million a month meant that we'd be able to pay for production for all the shows we'd dreamed up. We'd be able to hire people, shoot all this dope stuff. People were going to love it.

With numbers like that, I really thought we'd scale up in no time.

We knew we weren't going to beat Netflix or Hulu, okay, but we could become a real option for Black viewers and at least try to rival TV One or OWN. I may not have known much about the streaming game, but, by my math, if we were doing numbers to the tune of what I'd calculated, we could overcome whatever hurdles we encountered.

I couldn't have been more wrong. Even though I knew I didn't have much knowledge about streaming, it was only after we kicked off the app that I began to realize just how little I knew. In the worst miscalculation I possibly could've made, I unwittingly assumed that Vimeo calculated its numbers the same way YouTube did. Thus, I assumed that the forty-one thousand subscribers I was seeing were all *active* subscribers. Turned out, that number counted the *total number* of people who had ever signed up for the app, whether they were paying for it or not. Even if they'd just come to the app for a free trial and added their email, they were being counted. We actually had only about twenty thousand subscribers, less than half of what I'd originally believed. The other twenty thousand were folks who signed up for a free trial, watched whatever they could in that time, then canceled their subscription before the billing period started. Some of those same viewers would return, use a different email address to sign up for a free subscription, watch as much as they could at no cost, and then leave again.

In another equally egregious mistake, I assumed that we'd have to pay only sixty-five cents per subscriber to Vimeo and a five-cent transaction fee to process the new accounts. Thus, I assumed we'd be pocketing about $5.30 for every person who purchased a subscription to KevOnStage Studios. And this was indeed the case if our subscribers all signed up directly through the app. However, if they signed up on the Apple store or through Google Play, we'd have to fork over as much as 40 percent of that subscriber fee to Apple and Android. So now, instead of getting a little more than $5 a subscriber, we're only making about $3.80 per. Needless to say, with a subscriber base substantially smaller than I'd assumed, those figures didn't get us anywhere near a quarter million bucks a month.

Meanwhile, we had bills to pay. Equipment had to be bought and maintained. Actors and production teams had to be paid. It was the middle of the pandemic, so we had to pay for COVID testing and protocols designed to keep our workspaces safe. As if that wasn't enough, we wound up working with a producer who bilked us out of $100,000! (More on that in a minute.)

And what makes it all so bad is, people seemed to really love the shows! The average user watched a ton of them during the free trial period or the months when they paid for the service. We just couldn't get them to stick around and pay month after month like we needed. We also knew that password sharing was rampant. People wanted to watch what we were producing, but we never got a chance to get them in the habit of paying for what they saw. These are common problems for any streaming service, but the difference between those who can survive it and those who fold often comes down to having enough capital to fight through. We didn't have that.

We limped along as best we could for about four years, hoping that either we could change our subscribers' habits or we could find a buyer for the company who could infuse enough cash to keep us afloat. I knew we had a good idea. We just didn't have the money to last. As crazy as it sounds, I took pride in the fact that we were able to struggle along for as long as we did, even when companies that had much deeper pockets, like Quibi, were folding. Eventually, though, it became too much. I never regretted giving the app a try. But we were smart enough to know when it was finally over. We closed up KevOnStage Studios in 2024. So yeah, we lost that battle. But believe me, in our own ways, we continue to fight.

HOW I—AHEM—"MISMANAGED" $150,000

Truthfully, part of me doesn't want to tell this story at all. I mean, it's so embarrassing that I promised myself I'd only tell it if I was selling a book. It is 100 percent my fault. What's worse, none of it would have happened if I had listened to my wife. It represents the perfect combination of my ambition and my complete lack of patience—and it cost me at least $150K. (My wife puts the cost at $200K, which I refuse to accept simply because I can't stomach the idea of it.)

Here's a rundown of every mistake I made en route to losing that money, along with a handy list of do's and don'ts. I don't like rehashing this, you understand. I'm sharing this with you for one reason only: to help you avoid reaching this level of stupidity in your own life. Mind you, these mistakes are listed not necessarily in order of importance, but in order of appearance in this story.

———

Mistake 1: Hiring someone to do something without being certain that the person is known to do that thing well.

In case you didn't already know, being good at one thing doesn't automatically mean someone is good at something else.

The best thing you can do is to always check someone out thoroughly. Never neglect what we call "due diligence." You have someone's résumé? Read it carefully. You have his/her references? Check them all out diligently. Vet that person's work if possible. Know exactly who it is you're recruiting and what precisely it is that you need that person to do. Failure to do any of this was my first mistake.

This was back when I first started working on my TV series, *Churchy,* a comedy drama about a young minister who takes over a small church in rural Texas after he's rejected as a candidate to assume control over his dad's megachurch. As I was preparing to shoot, I reached out to someone about working on the series.

The job I was hiring them for was complex and important, and while I knew the person was good at one aspect of the job, I was looking for them to take on an expanded role. I didn't have a lot of money to shoot *Churchy.* And as anyone with any experience in film knows, the quickest way to blow a TV show budget is to fail to get filming done on any given day. I was desperate to avoid inefficiencies, and I assumed this person would be an ideal candidate for doing so.

I was happy to hear them tell me that with their experience and connections, the show could be completed for $250,000—half a million less than the budget we'd been cleared for! For all their skill, experience, and leverage, their asking price was only $3,000 and a producer's credit on the show.

"Let's do it!" I said.

Didn't check any references. Didn't call around. I just said, "Okay."

I love to give people opportunities, and in this business, it is especially hard for Black people to get fair chances. So I agreed to hire them, thinking I was gonna be the one to help another Black person get ahead.

Mistake 2: Failing to make sure all paperwork is signed *before* moving forward.

A legally binding document can offer you recourse if something goes haywire. But if it ain't signed, it's not legal. Do not move forward on a deal, a project, a partnership, or anything else until all paperwork is signed.

Why am I so insistent that you do this? Because I didn't.

My lawyer drafted the agreement between me and this person, but somehow, even though this person and I talked every day, I never double-checked that the electronic Docusign document was actually signed. Had I been more thorough, this signed agreement would've given me the option of taking that person to court if things went badly.

Picture my surprise when I realized we hadn't signed the deal. I'll help you out: It looked like me smacking myself in the head and saying *idiot* over and over.

Mistake 3: Ignoring my wife.

I did not listen to my wife. As egregious as Mistakes 1 and 2 were, this third one was the worst of all. (As I said before, these screw-ups are in order of appearance.)

We had a finance call with this person about how crew and actors would get paid. He had a finance production accountant on the line. (I did check the accountant's LinkedIn, and it matched up.) The two of them told us that the easiest way to handle disbursement of the money for the show would be to allocate $100,000 to them to pay for preproduction. This would go toward hiring crew members, buying insurance, renting trailers, and so forth. We'd hand over another $100,000 before the first week and the remainder of the money just before we wrapped the production. They would then deliver the actuals after all that.

When I used to oversee content for the All Def Digital brand, I handled productions this way all the time. But when I told my lovely and brilliant wife about the plan we'd devised on the call, she balked at the idea, saying that she'd feel more comfortable if she and I paid the people ourselves.

"It's a lot of money—and it's not that I don't trust y'all," she said, "but I would feel safer paying people myself."

Truth is, she didn't trust them and was wise enough to try to safeguard our investment. Unfortunately, I still had some hard lessons to learn.

Rather than agreeing, I assured Melissa that everything would be fine. She pushed back. I reassured her. She pushed back again. I reassured her again that everything was going to work out perfectly. Finally, she relented. Don't get me wrong: She didn't agree. She simply . . . gave in. To her, I was hell-bent on being an idiot, even though she'd tried to stop me. (Yes, you'd think I'd have learned my lesson about heeding Melissa's advice after the Poopgate incident that left me dropping a deuce in my pants on the bus ride to Tacoma years ago . . . but, hey, if nothing else, I'm consistent.) So instead of doing the smart thing like my wife wanted, we sent off three separate payments of $100,000 each.

To this day, I've never been given an accurate account of how that money was spent.

We did find out that not all of the actors were fully paid from that budget. Melissa and I wound up covering the differences by paying out of our pockets. Our Screen Actors Guild rep actually told us that we weren't legally required to pay the actors. Because we had paid the producer, SAG would go after this person. But we weren't even going to consider mistreating all the great people who'd worked so hard to make *Churchy* a success, so we stepped in personally. In addition to the actors, many members of the crew weren't paid for the final weeks—or at all—so, again, Melissa and I wound up paying with our own money. Also, because we were trying to do this in the middle of a once-in-a-lifetime pandemic, there was a $60,000 bill related to COVID-19 testing and social protocols that went unpaid from the budget. Melissa and I paid that, too.

Obviously, we lost a lot of money. Meanwhile, the production devolved into a whole mess by the last day. Things ended with this person threatening to fight another producer on the final day of shooting, and ultimately, we denied them the producer credit they had asked for. And all this nonsense—or at least the parts that sapped our show budget and left our personal bank account dented—could have been avoided if I had not made the mistakes I listed above, and most important, if I had actually listened to my wife.

Fortunately, we recovered and were still able to get *Churchy* made. Unfortunately, the project still nearly failed.

DON'T DO THE CRIME . . .
BECAUSE I WILL SNITCH

Hollywood can be a cutthroat place that brings out the worst in a lot of people. I'm sure it has everything to do with my upbringing, but I've never understood how some people can just steal from and swindle others, especially other people who are struggling just as badly or worse than you. And not only can I not mistreat someone that way, but if I find out you're out here doing wrong, please don't expect Kev to cover up for you—because I will most definitely tell.

Not too long ago, I saw a post on social media that asked, "If you were in the interrogation room, what meal would they have to bring you in order for you to snitch . . ."

Ha!

They'd have to bring me one single solitary Popeyes biscuit with some drink, and I'm telling on everybody. I'm telling everything. I know I look like a thug, but I'm really a church boy, like, a square. *I. Will. Tell. On. You.* For one McFlurry. One Chick-fil-A nugget with two dips of Polynesian sauce, and I'm telling on you.

An original Frosty from Wendy's? "It was him, your honor!" You understand me?

A catfish fillet fried good with three shakes of hot sauce? I'm gon' tell the crime.

Matter of fact, it don't have to be food. If I'm wearing socks and you dip my foot in water and you say, "Tell us everything, or you won't get fresh socks . . ."

Me: "Your honor, here's everything." Can't have my feet being wet.

You can let me watch two episodes of *The Office*—the basketball episode twice, actually—you let me watch that twice, I'm gon' tell them people on you.

A time machine to go back in time and get a Pizza Hut slice from 1992 paid for with coupons? I'm tellin' them folks on you. You understand me? It don't take much!

A strawberry lemonade from Red Robin, the Freckled Lemonade, and two of the steak fries. Matter of fact, steak fry and a half, I'm gon' tell them people about it. Oh yeahhhh.

One cinnamon bun. Matter of fact, one Auntie Anne's pretzel. "Your honor, it was Lil' Charlie."

CHURCHY

Although the streaming service would eventually die an ugly death, KevOnStage Studios still enabled me to realize one of my most elusive dreams. As the app reeled and our team scrambled unsuccessfully to find new sources of revenue, I threw up one final Hail Mary attempt to win subscribers and make us some money. I created, and aired on our app, my first-ever TV show.

Based very loosely on my experiences growing up in church in El Paso, *Churchy* is a comedy series that follows an up-and-coming young minister, Corey Carr, Jr. (played by me), who moves to Lubbock, Texas, to start a church after his dad, a megachurch pastor, rejects Corey as his successor. Corey is determined to prove to his father (played by my original comedy inspiration, Jonathan Slocumb) that he's more than capable enough to lead a flock, so he tries to build his own ministry from scratch.

Even though KevOnStage Studios was burning through much of its cash, we were blessed to get a huge lift from an unexpected source.

None other than basketball icon LeBron James, along with his friend and business partner Maverick Carter, took a liking to the idea behind *Churchy* and agreed to produce the show through their entertainment company, SpringHill. Melissa and I served as executive producers. (Jason, who was alive for the first season of the show, received an executive producer credit and still gets one posthumously.) I'd worked with the team at SpringHill on previous projects, most notably a short-lived TV show called *Crossover*, and had built up enough rapport with executives that they were willing to take a chance on *Churchy*. I had no idea then if it'd be enough to save the streaming service. But we'd created the app to pursue our wildest creative dreams in the first place; if KevOnStage Studios was going to go down, we'd go down doing the work that made us happy.

We did go down. Although the show debuted on the app in early 2024, we knew after a couple of months that not even *Churchy* was going to be able to lift us out of the financial hole we'd fallen into.

But thanks to that show, good fortune found us, too. Not long before we shut down our streaming app, we managed to cut a deal with Black Entertainment Television (BET) to move *Churchy* over to the BET+ streaming service, where it still airs. In one of our last acts as platform executives, we not only struck an eleventh-hour deal that gave us enough of a financial boost to wriggle out of some of the debt we'd accumulated, but we also managed to breathe new life into exactly the sort of creative effort we'd founded the studio to tackle to begin with. In our own way, we'd closed an important circle.

In February 2024, with the show set to premiere on "real TV" in a matter of days, I found myself in New York City to watch the unveiling of a billboard in Times Square for *Churchy*. Originally I'd flown in to do one of the tour dates for the Bald Brothers show, but the network and Paramount wanted to make sure I got a chance to see the advertisement. Even before I got to New York, I'd made plans to head over to see the billboard by myself and then leave quickly. But by the time I found myself standing at the intersection of Broadway, Seventh Avenue, and Forty-second Street looking up at the Manhattan skyline that wintry February fourth, I wasn't alone.

Unbeknownst to me, some of my closest family and friends had flown in as a surprise. Along with my comedic partner and tourmate Tony, there was my wife and co-author Melissa, the wise and long-suffering military brat who'd accompanied me to the seminal *Kings of Comedy* movie on our third date nearly a quarter-century ago and who'd raised two wonderful boys all while nurturing my crazy ambitions. Tami, Jason's wife, had flown out with her two daughters, too. To my delight, they'd also made the surprise journey with my now teenage sons, once budding internet darlings and YouTube sensations whose big breaks had given me the courage to make my own.

Oblivious to the cold, the crowds, and the roaring New York traffic, we stood out there and gazed up for long minutes as the billboard promoting my first-ever TV show was uncovered. All of us had traveled a long, sometimes tortuous road over the past decade and a half to be here. For my part, I'd walked away from decent jobs and the promise of steady middle-class comfort. I'd bombed out of comedy shows, been booed off stand-up stages, and been booted out of some of the hottest digital companies of the day. I had endured criticisms that I wasn't funny, that I wasn't edgy enough for modern comedy, that all I could talk about was church. I'd lost paychecks. I'd lost opportunities. I'd lost my only brother. Even after I'd hit it big, I still stumbled, squandering money on useless producers and now-dead phone apps.

But you know what? I was good with all that. Because even if I may not have been the hottest comedian or the best playwright, I'd endured. I had stayed the course. I had faced all the harsh judgments, all the catcalls and boos, all my own fears that I might not make it, and I'd proven I could rise above it all. I'd learned that winners aren't always victorious, and that losers don't always have to embrace defeat. Whether I'd walked tall or tumbled onto my face, I had always found a way to keep moving ahead. I didn't care if I flopped, as long as I gave my best effort. I'd proven that I could find the way ahead regardless.

In that moment in the middle of Times Square, as with much of my life before and since, I was perfectly fine being a successful failure.

ACKNOWLEDGMENTS

I want to thank my wife, Melissa, for being the most instrumental part of my journey in my life. I love you.

My sons, Isaiah and Josiah, make me proud to be their father every single day. I love you both.

To my family, for being the basis of my being. I love you all.

To Darrell Dawsey, my writer for this book, my partner in literary crime, I couldn't have done this without your amazing work. Thank you.

ABOUT THE AUTHOR

KEVIN FREDERICKS is an NAACP Image Award–winning comedian, the founder of KevOnStage Studios, a bestselling author, and a superstar on social media. His work and commentary have been featured by *Good Morning America, Complex, Ebony, Newsweek, The Daily Beast,* and MSNBC.

kevonstage.com
X: @kevonstage
Instagram: @kevonstage